I0440972

SMALL TOWN AMERICA
Families along the Chippewa River

NUSSBERGER – BOEHM

BY

ARTHUR A. NUSSBERGER

Copyright © 2007 by Arthur A. Nussberger. 35491-NUSS
Library of Congress Control Number: 2006908499
ISBN: Softcover   978-1-4257-3464-0

All rights reserved. No part of this book may be reproduced
or transmitted in any form or by any means, electronic or
mechanical, including photocopying, recording, or by any
information storage and retrieval system, without permission
in writing from the copyright owner.

Print information available on the last page

Book Designer: Alfred B. Ilagan

To order additional copies of this book, contact:
Xlibris
1-888-795-4274
www.Xlibris.com
Orders@Xlibris.com

Chippewa Valley from Chippewa Falls to Durand, Wisconsin
Durand located in Pepin County along the banks of the Chippewa River [1]

Part 1. *Early Pioneers ...*

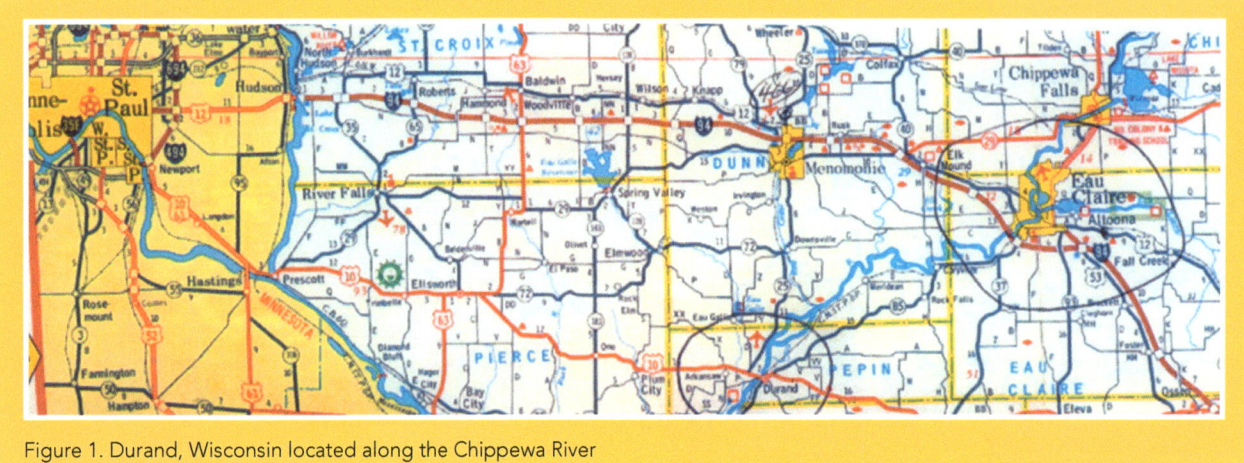

Figure 1. Durand, Wisconsin located along the Chippewa River

The Chippewa Valley opened for lumbering following the treaty of 1837 between the U.S. and the Chippewa (Ojibwe) Indians. The white pine forests became a resource and the Chippewa River was a natural transportation link for the production of lumber. Under Articles contained in the treaty of 1837 the Chippewa nation ceded land that included the Chippewa Valley to the United States. The Valley was described as extending a half days march below the fall on the Chippewa River. My great Grandparents (Nussberger) were immigrants from Germany and arrived in Durand, Wisconsin, Pepin County, about the time of the 1837 treaty (Fig. 1). In exchange for the ceded land the U.S. government paid the Chippewa nation $9,500 annually for a term of 20 years, approximately $196,000 in money and goods to establish 3 blacksmith shops, deliver farm goods, provide for half breeds, and settle claims against the Chippewa nation. The Indians were granted privileges of hunting, fishing, and gathering wild rice on the land.

Lumber dominated the economy of the Valley for 40 years (Fig. 2). Villages grew into towns as thousands of settlers poured into the Valley. The lumber economy created many business opportunities e.g. my father's blacksmith shop.

The early Nussberger family is believed to be among the first white settlers in Pepin County. The original stone cabin, built in 1846 and occupied by the Nussberger's as their home, is still in existence (Figs.3 and 4). The cabin was located on thousands of acres homesteaded and extending for nearly five miles to the present southern town limits of Durand, Wisconsin. After settling on the land and living there for many years, the land was finally deeded to my Grandfather, Conrad Nussberger, under provisions of the Federal Land Grant Act of 1864. The original deed has the signature of President Chester Arthur. Townspeople have speculated that Congress approved the land grants as a settlement to veterans of the civil war.

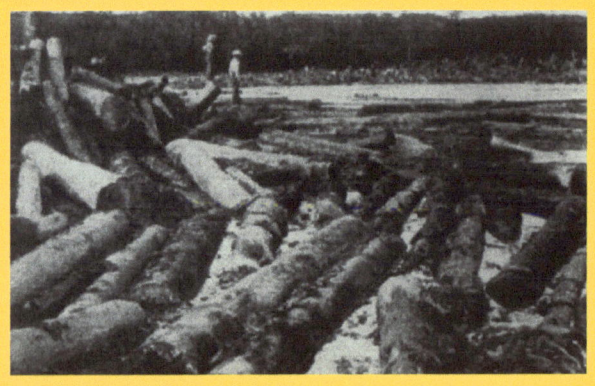

Figure 2. Logging on the Chippewa River

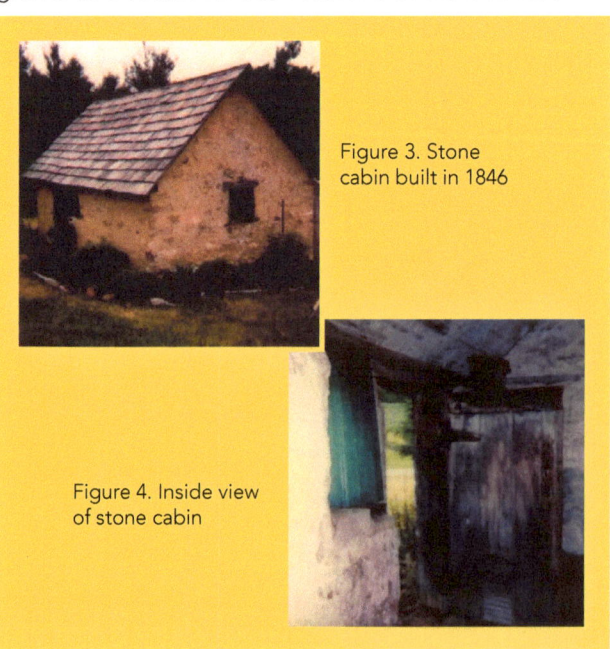

Figure 3. Stone cabin built in 1846

Figure 4. Inside view of stone cabin

---

1 The story material is mainly from memory and newspaper accounts of events. Some important information was obtained from a family book and tree provided by Angela Boehm, a first cousin, and compiled by Marilyn Erickson.

Andrew Nussberger Sr. the early years...

My father Andrew Nussberger Sr. was born December 15, 1885 the son of Conrad and Caroline Black Nussberger (Fig. 5). Caroline died following Andrew's birth. His father (affectionately referred to by friends as "Coon") remarried shortly thereafter and Andrew soon had two stepbrothers and one stepsister. He also lived in a new house that "Coon" built for his new wife. Andrew's Grandmother thought he was being mistreated by the new mother and couldn't stand the perceived mistreatment. She moved young Andrew into the stone cabin with her and raised him. My great Grandmother continued living in that old stone cabin until her death. She was without a husband since before Andrew had been born. Her husband was killed in a dynamite explosion while mining limestone on the property. As the surviving son, "Coon" claimed inheritance to the homestead. Andrew grew up doing farm chores along side his dad. At the age of 15, in the year 1900, Andrew left the family homestead and went out on his own.

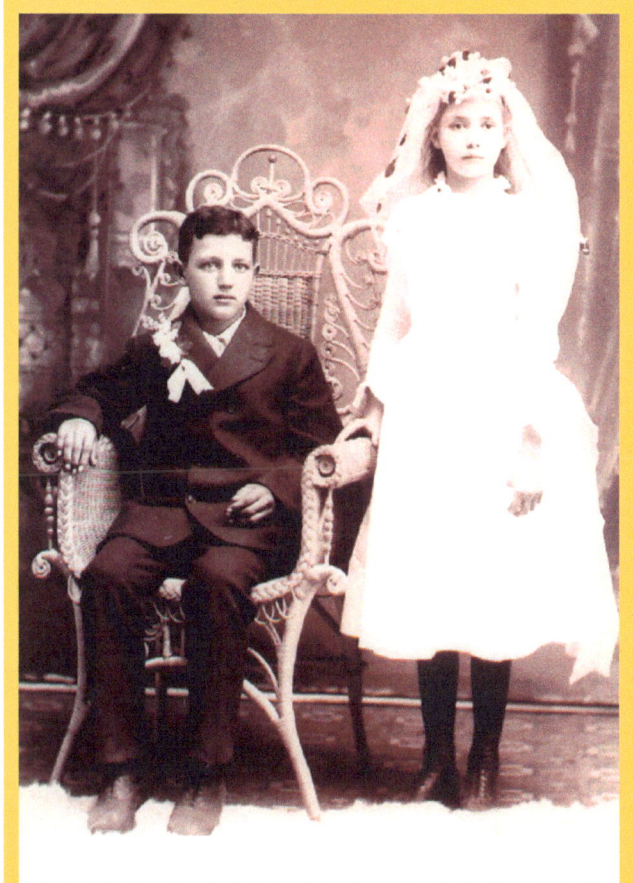

Figure 5. Andrew Sr. with cousin Clara age 10

Andrew Nussberger started working in a blacksmith shop...

After leaving home Andrew's ambition was to become a railroad engineer. He started along that path by taking a correspondence course and working as a fireman on one of the local trains. Andrew soon discovered that he was colorblind and would never be allowed to run the locomotive. He gave up on a career

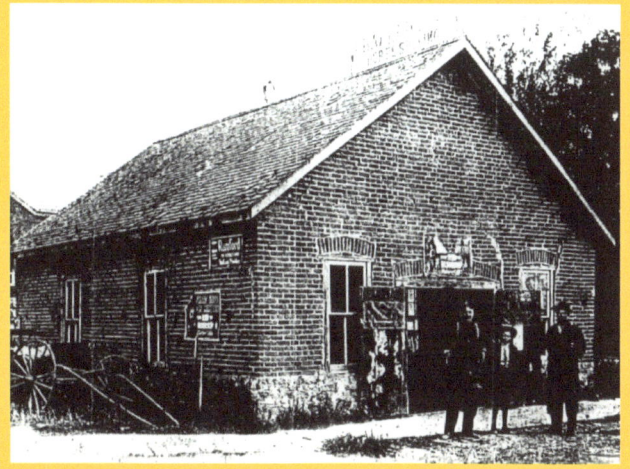

Figure 6. Andrew started working in blacksmith shop in 1900

with the railroad and started working in a blacksmith shop shoeing horses (Fig. 6). In the evenings he would work in the local movie house as the film projectionist. Andrew grew up in an early pioneer family and was used to rough living. He liked gambling and at times drinking. But, In spite of this, Andrew was well liked in the community and gained a reputation for honesty and hard work. During his youth Andrew was an excellent swimmer and once was credited with saving the life of his cousin while they were swimming in the Chippewa River bordering Durand.

Agnes Boehm's family...

Andrew's future wife, Agnes Boehm (my mother), was the daughter of Dominic Boehm and Rosalie Bauer Boehm (Fig. 7). Agnes grew up on a farm as the second youngest in a family of ten children. She was extremely proud of her dad (my Grandfather) and admired him for leading 85 people to this new country from Austria.

Dominic Boehm was born in Schrems, Austria, August 4, 1844, son of Tobias and Eva Boehm. There were six other sons besides Dominic. They all stayed in Austria and are buried in Schrems, Austria. Dominic had witnessed the turmoil of war and had been part of a burial party for dead Austrian soldiers killed near Vienna during the Prussian- Austrian war. America

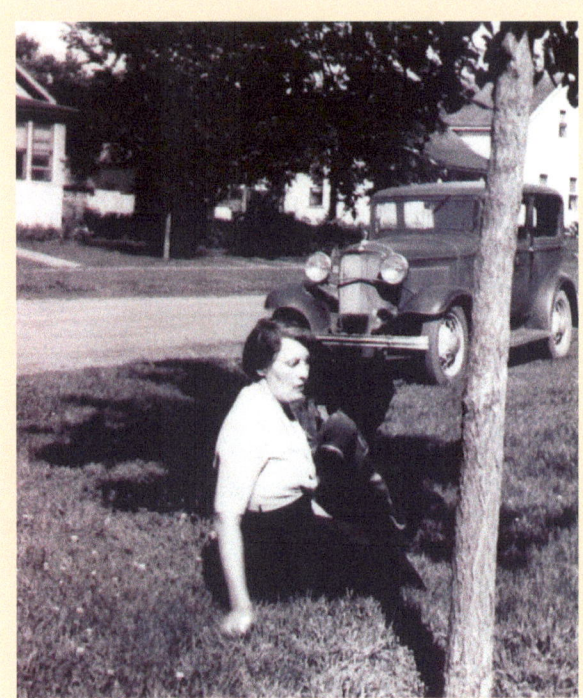

Figure 7. Agnes Boehm Nussberger about 1932

offered new opportunities. He came to the United States in 1865 and worked in Eau Claire, Wisconsin as a shoemaker until 1871. In 1871, he cut his hand and the Doctor told him that he wouldn't be able to work for some months. During the period of recovery, he took the opportunity and returned to Schrems, Austria to visit his family. While visiting his parents, the news got out and spread throughout the town that there was an American visiting. Townspeople were eager to hear about this new country from one of their own that had lived there. Dominic described the opportunities and gave them answers that satisfied their fears including fears about being killed by Indians. Dominic explained that there was plenty of farmland available at little or no cost and only required a skill at farming and a willingness to work hard. These Austrian people were good farmers and hard workers. Grandpa led them to the Durand area because Wisconsin was a new state and offered cheap farmland to immigrants.

The ocean voyage to America was still an adventure and very dangerous. Dominic's first voyage to America in 1865 had been on a sailing ship and the trip lasted 13 weeks. The ship carried food and water provisions for only 6 weeks. Half way through the voyage mutiny occurred with many of the passengers wanting to return to Austria. The captain realized that they were at the point of no return, i.e., as far back to Austria as to New York. The captain used armed force to stop the mutiny and the passengers survived by strict rationing. The crew worked around the clock to repair sails and everyone helped to row the ship to New York. Some of the weaker passengers died during the voyage and all suffered near starvation.

Dominic helped the captain in turning back the mutiny and the captain took a liking to Dominic and taught him to read and write English. Dominic's second trip to America, leading 85 immigrants, was by steamship. Dominic later learned that on the return voyage the ship sank and all hands were lost. The group had varying economic backgrounds and some families were much better off financially than others. Dominic would negotiate the group lodging and meals and ask the better off ones to pay more than an equal share to make it easier on the poorer families. The wealthier people objected to paying more and in the streets of New York Dominic had a revolt of his own. Dominic called their bluff by telling them that if they did not like it they could go their separate way. He started down the street with the rebellious group standing and watching him depart. As he got a few blocks away the group panicked and ran to catch up.

Most of the new immigrants wore rough clothing, which easily marked them as fresh off the boat. These people were Catholic and on Sunday Dominic took them to St. Patrick's Cathedral to worship holy mass. They sat in the last few rows of the church and some smart aleck kids would walk behind them and chalk their backs. The kids judged the immigrants by their clothes and the immigrants didn't understand what was going on. Grandpa Boehm knew better and when it was his turn to get chalked he was ready and the kids got a good cuffing and it was the end to the practice of chalking.

One of the families that came with Dominic was Michael and Barbara Bauer from Clayburn, Austria. They had four sons and 2 daughters including a daughter named Rosalie. Dominic was 27 years old and still unmarried. Rosalie was pretty and just 21 at the time having been born on September 4, 1850.

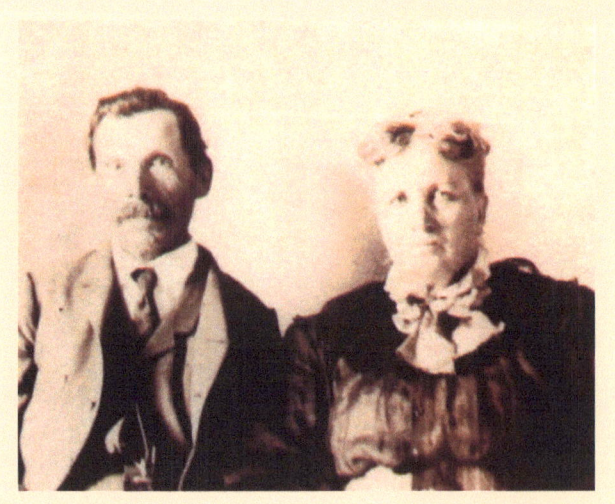

Figure 8. Maternal grandparents Dominic and Rosalie Boehm

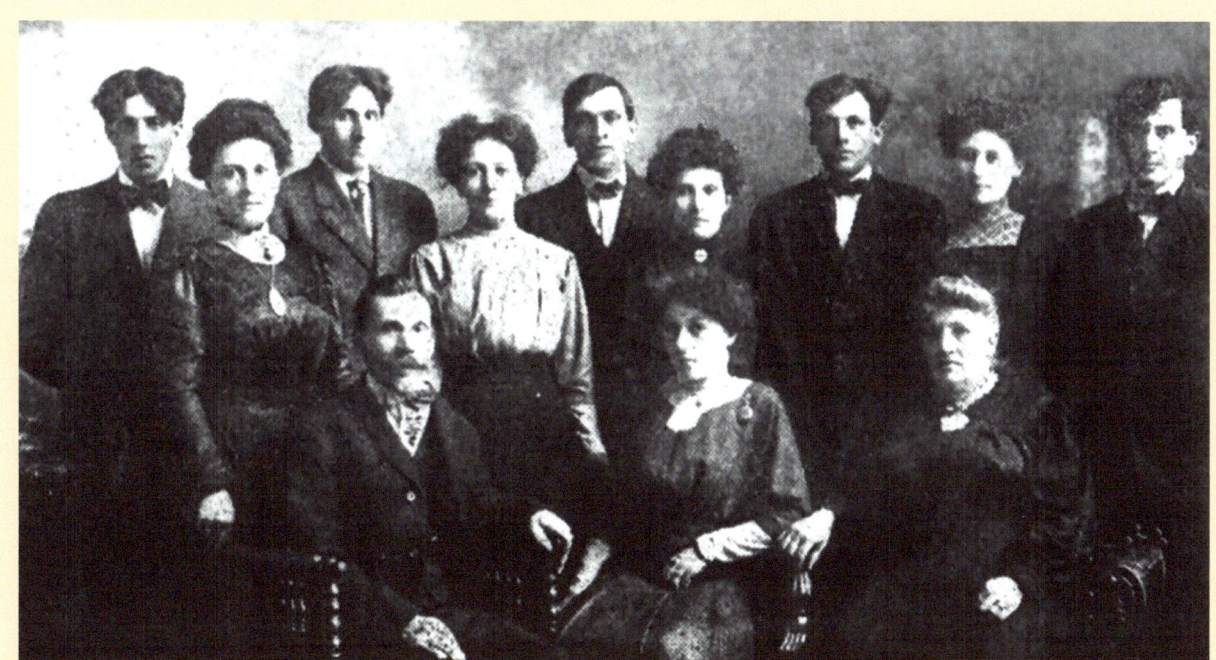

Figure 9. Dominic and Rosalie Boehm and their 10 children
(back row Robert, Henry, John, Thomas, Ignatius; middle row Mary, Louise, Rose, Agnes; front row Dominic, Anna and Rosalie)

A sea voyage is especially conducive toward making young people more romantic and they developed a shipboard romance. Dominic waited until all of the immigrant families were settled before he and Rosalie were married (Fig. 8). The marriage took place on July 29, 1873. Ten children resulted from this union, five boys and five girls, including my mother. After there marriage, Mr. And Mrs. Boehm lived in Mondovi, Wisconsin for three years, where he worked at the trade he learned as a young man, shoemaking. Later they settled outside Durand, Wisconsin and developed a prosperous farm overlooking the Chippewa River on 600 acres of rich farmland. The Boehm farm was located across the river from Durand. At the time there was a toll charge to cross the river bridge into downtown Durand. The toll was 10 cents if you walked and 15 cents for horse and buggy.

The Boehm family was a large musical family (Fig. 9). Dominic played the piano and my mother Agnes played the piano. Her brother John, the 2nd oldest, played the violin. Together they often hosted parties and played for dances. My mother grew up in this large musical family.

The oldest child was Rosalie (Aunt Rose) born September 25, 1874 and died August 7, 1966. She married Michael Resler on May 23, 1893 and they also had 10 children. Two of her children, Joseph and Felix, I remember well. After Aunt Rose's husband died she went to live with them on a farm outside Neillsville, Wisconsin. Both Joseph and Felix remained unmarried and were gentle people and wouldn't hurt a fly. Even though deer hunting was a favorite sport in this part of the state they never took part. Joe and Felix would never kill a deer but enjoyed the exploits of the hunters. They loved to tell stories about friends

and relatives that stayed at their farm to go deer hunting. Near by one of Aunt Rose's daughters had a strawberry farm and once each summer we would spend a Sunday visiting at Joe and Felix's and on the way home stop at the strawberry farm and pick up crates of strawberries. The next day we would be busy picking over and canning strawberries.

John was the next oldest and with mother enjoyed playing the violin. The third born was Mary. She was a strong individualist. Aunt Mary had been married twice, first to Sebastain Baur who died at the age of 38 years and next to Frank Magadance. After her second husband died at the age of 47 in 1924, Mary was left with two small children to raise as a single parent. Frank Magadance had been a businessman and owned and operated a tomb stone business. There was a sizable debt for her to pay off and she had to learn how to cope with this burden. Over the years she converted low cost houses into rooming homes and rentals in Eau Claire, Wisconsin and became quite wealthy. She was adventurous and once rode a motorcycle across the width of Wisconsin. She also once owned and operated a country tavern and store in a very rural and rough part of Wisconsin. The next oldest was Louise. Louise's husband died at an early age while in the dentist chair having a tooth extracted. Both her brothers Hank and Rob told stories about a spirit appearing on the night of his death at their farmhouse doorstep and asking for help. The boys were so frightened and they couldn't understand what it was that the spirit wanted and the spirit slowly disappeared. No one knows if it was true or not but it's certain Hank and Rob believed that it had happened.

My mother's brother Ignatius (I.G.) was born January 2, 1881. After trying to support nine children on a farm and already in his mid 40's he made a career change and started selling health and accident insurance policies for Woodman Insurance Company of Lincoln, Nebraska. Ignatius was a born salesman and soon so successful that he was promoted to supervisor of the Wisconsin territory. Ignatius was given credit for saving the company with his sales. He once told me of the time when the Company President invited him to visit in Lincoln, Nebraska. Ignatius was terrified about going to Lincoln since he expected to be fired from his salesman job. He had reasoned that his poor penmanship on the application forms was not acceptable. Ignatius had little formal education. At the home office the President of the Company told him not to worry about penmanship since they had many college graduates to straighten out the applications. They wanted him to attend sales motivation meetings across the country and give the salesmen a motivating talk. Ignatius was shocked and questioned, "What would I tell them?" The President said, "Just tell them how you started from such a humble beginning and succeeded through determination and hard work." Ignatius agreed to give the speech and went to Chicago for his first meeting. The speaker in front of him was a supervisor and University educated. This speaker bored the audience and there was only polite applause. Ignatius got up and gave his speech and the house came alive and he got a standing ovation.

The fifth born was Robert. He was another gifted orator and could have easily passed for a preacher. He married Appalonia Dahlke on November 24, 1914 and everyone called her Lonnie. Robert made his living farming and was an excellent farmer. I remember Uncle Rob visiting us one fall at our home in Durand after he had spent the summer working in the fields. He was about 75 years old and looked bronze and the picture of health.

Henry was next in age and an easygoing type of person. Like his brothers, Uncle Hank as he was called, made his living by farming. In his later years Uncle Hank would auction off all the livestock in the fall and close up his farm and spend the winter in Florida. In the spring he would return and restock and farm until fall. In the early 1940's we were invited to his first retirement party. Driving to Halder to attend the party our 1937 Studebaker broke down. Dad flagged a motorist and got him to pull us into the nearest garage. Parts were scarce since this was during the World War and the next morning Dad went to the garage and using their lathe machined out the necessary parts.

Thomas followed Henry in age but I never got to know him. Our mother Agnes was next born November 8, 1891. Mother never liked living on a

farm and was one of the few members of her family that settled in town. The last of the Boehm children was Anna born in 1893. Her husband, Joseph, owned a farm in Halder, Wisconsin and operated the local creamery. Most of the Boehm family settled around Halder on farms. During the depression of the 1930's there was a lot of feuding between the farmers and the creameries over milk prices. Blockages and strikes occurred and Joseph and the Boehm brothers were on opposite sides of the issue.

The Boehm children grew up on the banks of the Chippewa River and learned farming from their dad. During these years the family was very close. As they were growing up the Boehm family suffered through a catastrophic fire that destroyed the house, which was later rebuilt. The Boehm boys had their individual rivalries. Henry and Robert seemed to be keen rivals throughout their lives. During their adult years they lived on adjacent farms in Halder and they never tired of telling stories about which was the better farmer. Mother was fond of stories about them as boys. It seems that one of Robert's tasks was to bring in the firewood from outdoors during the cold winter and start the early morning fire. Henry had a habit of gargling and spitting on the firewood. This annoyed Robert and one night after a late dance Henry came home and as usual gargled. This time the water pitcher was filled with kerosene and he gargled with the kerosene and that ended the habit of Henry gargling and spitting on the firewood. Grandpa Boehm was strict and no nonsense, so the boys couldn't make any disturbance and just went to bed.

As the boys became adults, Grandpa Boehm sold his farm and staked each of the boys to $1000 for down payments to buy their own farms. Ignatius (who hated the name and later insisted on being called I.G.) had visited his girl friend in an area around Mosinee, Wisconsin; a rural community called Halder, about 100 miles east of Durand. He wanted to get married and settle there and talked the other brothers into doing the same. Halder is where John, Thomas, Robert, Henry and Ignatius settled. Later Anna married and also settled in Halder. They all spent most of their years wishing they had stayed and settled in the Durand area. Halder was located in the middle of the state and had very short summers and long winters. The land was hard to farm and it wasn't always very profitable. The boys were dairy farmers and work was hard requiring early morning and late evening milking of the dairy cows and long summer days in the fields. The depression came along and they felt trapped. Later as a result of World War II, prices escalated and the Boehm's all made good on their farms and paid off their mortgages.

Grandpa and Grandma Boehm had promised the boys that they would spend one year in Halder with them and get them started. After the one-year they moved back to Durand and retired to the small house built adjoining our family home. This made it easier for mother and dad to look out for them. Grandpa and Grandma Boehm celebrated their 50th wedding anniversary on July 29, 1923. At the time of their 50th there were 48 grandchildren and two great grandchildren. The city council was kind enough to make the fair grounds available to accommodate the large crowd of celebrants. It was a big celebration in Durand with over 500 people attending. Many of these were the family members of the original group led over by Grandpa Boehm. Their grandchildren and great and great great grandchildren are still numbered among Durand's leading citizens.

The Courting of Agnes Boehm ...

Andrew started courting Agnes Boehm in 1908, eight years after he had left home. By this time Durand had grown from a logging settlement into a prosperous small town. Most of the townspeople made their living by providing goods and services to the farm family's who would come to town on Saturday

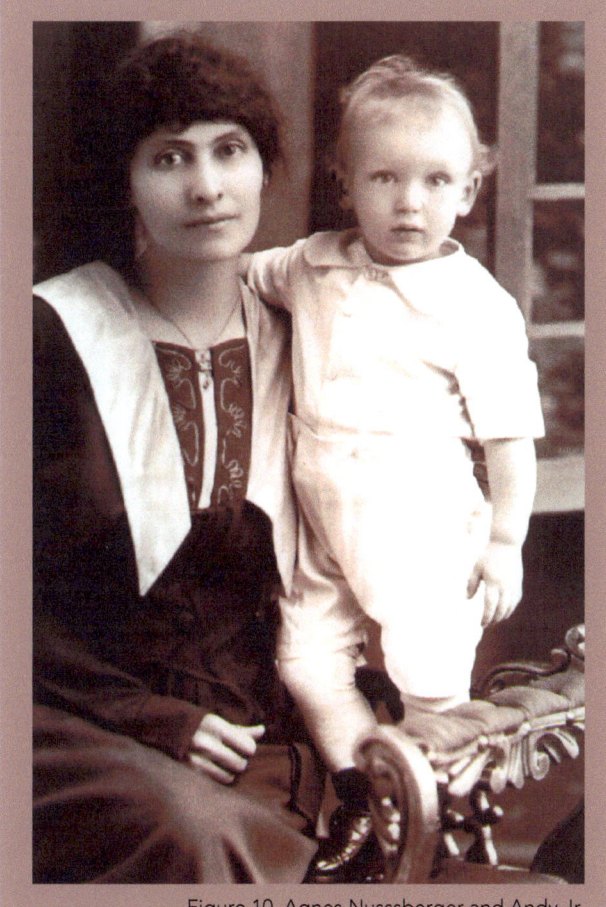

Figure 10. Agnes Nusssberger and Andy Jr.

night. The farmwomen did the shopping while the men unwound by visiting and drinking in the local taverns. Agnes was one month short of her 20th birthday when she married Andrew on October 24, 1911 (Fig. 10). Agnes' father liked Andrew and considered him to be honest, hard working and religious (all very much the characteristics favored by Austrian parents). Agnes was raised on a farm and determined that she would not live on a farm after her marriage. One of the conditions of the marriage was that they live in town and that Andrew no longer gamble or drink. Andrew agreed and remained faithful to these promises for the rest of his life.

Shortly after the turn of the century Andrew started working as a blacksmith and horseshoer in Durand. In 1912 he built a large brick shop building at the south end of Main Street and opened his own horse shoeing business (Fig. 11). The building stood

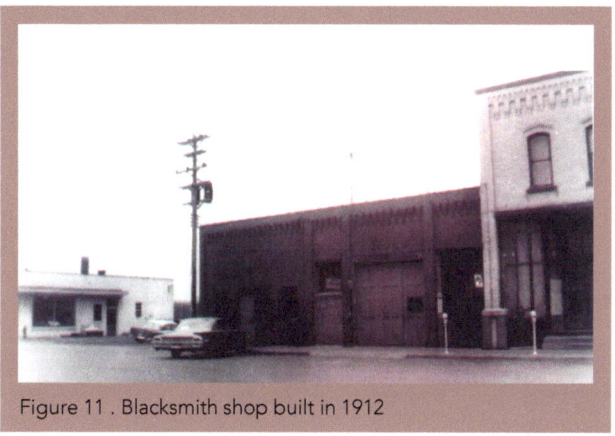

Figure 11 . Blacksmith shop built in 1912

until a fire destroyed it in 1973. In 1912, Andrew's business was prospering and the Nussbergers built their first house. With help from Agnes' uncle (who was a carpenter) they were able to construct a large two-story frame house on land located on the south edge of town, within walking distance of their parish church and school. The parcel of land was large enough to permit construction of a small house for Agnes' parents. About that time, Andrew's dad sold the deeded homestead farm and retired on a small house located along the riverbank and within sight of Andrew's home. Andrew and Agnes Nussberger were now settled in their own home and within easy walking distance of both their aging parents.

Through Dad's hard work and long hours, the blacksmith shop prospered and Andrew was able to hire several employees. Both Andrew and Agnes had little formal education, only enough to learn to read,do arithmetic, and write. Andrew educatedhimself to manage his business and later

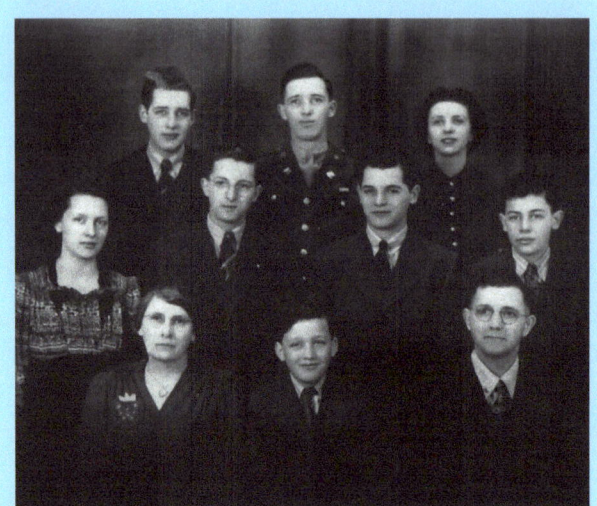

Figure 12. Andrew and Agnes Nussberger family in 1941 (back row Hubert, Andy Jr., Adeline; middle row Ruth, Harry, Donald, Arthur; front row Agnes, Ronald, Andrew Sr.)

Agnes and Andrew's family ...

Agnes was a devoted homemaker and took great pride in her children. Her eight children were about 3 years apart in ages. Adeline is the oldest, born in 1912, followed by Ruth, Andrew Jr., Hubert, Donald, Harry, Arthur, and Ronald, the youngest born in 1932. Agnes and Andrew Nussberger raised their family in the rural town of Durand, Wisconsin. These two people, both born in the 19th Century, lived through the Spanish-American War, World War 1, survived the flu epidemic of 1918 and the great depression of the 1930's, lived through World War 2 and raised 8 children without government assistance programs (Fig. 12). This was a time when rugged individuality was the accepted way of life. For over 60 years Andrew made his living by working 6 days a week in the "shop."

Shortly after his marriage, Andrew (Fig. 13) was elected to the city council and participated in the creation of a canning factory for the local pea and

converted the blacksmith and horse shoeing shop into a modern machine and repair business. He taught himself the skills necessary to do gas and electric welding, forging, lathe, milling, and shaper machine operations, thread cutting, trip hammer operation, and farm machinery repair. Andrew was intelligent and good at mathematics. There wasn't a time that the farmers in the area ever brought in a job that he couldn't figure out a way to help them. During the summer months the shop was always a beehive of activities. Andrew would be working on more than one job at a time with farmers (customers) working right along side. In the summer, the farmers were always in a hurry for their repairs since the breakdowns always seemed to occur right in the middle of planting or harvesting.

During the summer Andrew's day began at 6 o'clock with breakfast and ended around 10 o'clock at night. He would come home around 12 noon for lunch and again at 6 o'clock for an evening meal. Andrew spent the rest of the day and evening working in the "shop". Andrew's meals were always the same. He never ate corn and seldom ate potatoes or meat. Each meal consisted of eggs, oatmeal or cream of wheat, rice, prunes, milk, water, and bread. Andrew had an artesian well at the house and always carried drinking water to the shop since the city water contained large quantities of rust. On Sunday, he would attend early mass at Saint Mary's Church and then relax for a couple of hours reading the paper and listening to religious sermons on the radio. In the afternoon he would do repair chores around the house or at the shop. During the winter months it was less demanding and often business was too slow since most of the farm repair work occurred during the summer months. The farm equipment repair business was always good during depression years when farmers had little money for new equipment.

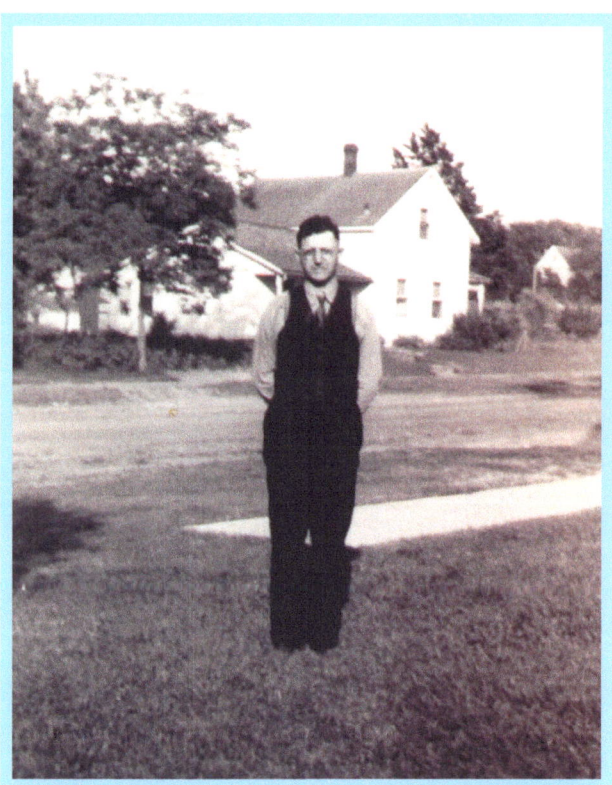

Figure 13. Andrew Nussberger Sr. neighbor's house in background

bean crops. His investment was modest but its success encouraged him to look for more ways to invest. Andrew tried to help his children whenever possible. When Andy Jr. was 16, Dad financed his first truck and later helped Andy to obtain a contract with the city to maintain the roads in and around Durand. Shortly before Pearl Harbor and the start of the Second World War, for the United States, Dad shopped around to buy a theater for Andy to operate. This was a great investment idea but the war interfered and Andy enlisted into the army. After the war ended Dad helped Andy and Harry open a new Gamble-Skogmo store in Pardeeville, Wisconsin. Andrew had hopes that his son's would join him in the shop and always had a sign over the entrance that read **"ANDREW NUSSBERGER and SONS"**.

Agnes had an outgoing personality and loved to talk about her childhood. It seemed that all of the Boehm's were great talkers. Many evenings Uncle I. G. would visit and talk for hours and we would listen spellbound. When Uncle I.G. got to the good part of a funny story he would revert to German, which the kids didn't understand. During one of these visits, Uncle I. G. was talking and Dad closed his eyes and dozed off. Uncle I.G. noticed that he was napping and commented, ***"The poor man works hard and is very tired"*** and then went right on talking. A few minutes later Dad awoke and listened as though nothing out of the ordinary happened.

Agnes and Andrew lived their entire lives in and around Durand and rarely traveled further than 100 miles from their home. They were both keenly interested in knowing about outside events and took great interest in national politics and followed daily news stories in newspaper and radio reports and later television. Their major travels consisted of a trip, about 1938, to Chicago to attend the world's fair during the summer of 1933 and a trip to St. Louis in 1942 to visit Andrew Jr. who was stationed at Scott Air Force Base near St. Louis. The world fair trip was taken with Ruth and her husband Kenneth as part of a wedding honeymoon. Local trips were mainly an occasional summer Sunday automobile drive to Halder for a Boehm family gathering. We would get up early on Sunday morning, attend 6 o'clock mass, eat breakfast and make the two-hour drive to Halder. As kids, we always looked forward to stopping on the way home and Dad buying us ice cream cones. The family gathering was always a lot of fun and included a tour of the farm, lively round table discussions of politics with many opposing views, and lots of good things to eat and drink. Dad and Mother looked forward to these visits and very much enjoyed the day. Andrew loved fairs and circuses and each year he would take us to those events. Aunt Mary worked the local fairs with a hamburger stand and we would see her at the fairs. She had a Franklin automobile with a rumble seat and a jawbreaker machine on each of the rear fenders. One afternoon she was visiting us in Durand and Harry and I broke into the jawbreakers. I was about 5 years old at the time and when Aunt Mary found out about it

she asked if we wanted more jawbreakers? I fell for the "trap" and she grabbed me and gave me a good swat and said, "Here is your jaw breaker!" Harry was a little older and a little smarter and never got the swat. Mother always felt that Aunt Mary held it against Harry that he never got swatted.

Part 2. *Devoted Son and Brother...*

In early1941 the United States was preparing for entry into World War II and Andy Jr. had already enlisted into the Army Air Force (Fig.14).

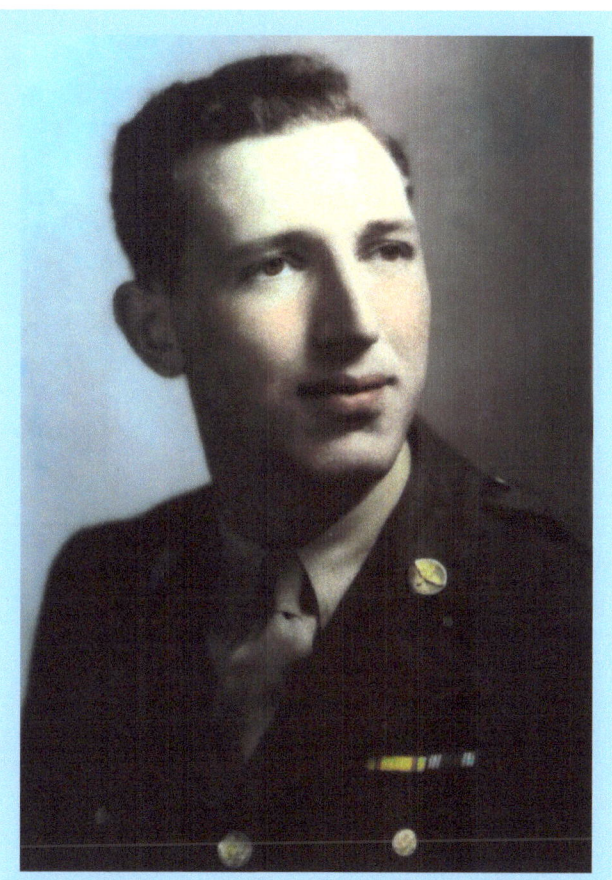

Figure 14. Andy Jr. in 1941

When Andy enlisted into the Army in 1941 he had his trucking business (two trucks) and had a contract with the city of Durand to provide road service and maintenance. He also had a license to haul cattle and did so, to the St. Paul stockyard. During these early years Andy was well known and liked in Durand. He worked hard and did an exceptionally good job maintaining the roads in and around Durand. This was a difficult task particularly in the winter with the snow. Andy was always prompt and kept the city roads plowed and clean and the people of Durand recognized and were appreciative of this service. Dad helped him buy his first truck and Andy always appreciated this help. After Andy went into the service, Hubert maintained the contract with the city for a while, but then Hubert went to Milwaukee to work as a welder for the Heil Company doing defense work. At this time Andy and Dad decided that the best thing to do was sell the trucks and licenses.

The day before Andy had to report for the army he visited Adeline in Halder, Wisconsin and stayed over night. The next day Mark drove him to Wausaw and he left by train to go to St. Louis where he was stationed at Scott Field. When he returned after 3 1/2 years in the pacific area the first place he stopped was in Omaha where Adeline and Mark were then living. He stayed over night and then went on home to Durand. After Harry got back from the Army he and Andy visited Adeline in Omaha. Adeline remembers the day that Mark, Andy, and Harry stopped at a bar and they questioned Harry's age.

Andy's 1936 Ford station wagon...

Andy bought a 1936 Ford station wagon and often drove home for weekends from Scott Field near St. Louis, a distance of about 550 miles. Andy would carry other soldiers as passengers to share the expense and drop them off along the way. The station wagon didn't have much of a heater and in the winter it was cold driving. Andy would partition the front seat off and get a little more heat that way. Most of the time at home would be spent getting the station wagon in shape for the drive back to the air base. Andy was home on a weekend pass on Pearl Harbor day December 7, 1941. We heard the news from the radio of the Japanese attack and like everyone else wondered just what it would mean. Our lives would never be the same after Pearl Harbor. Shortly after the Japanese attack, Andy was transferred to West Palm Beach, Florida for more training. We didn't see him for some time but always received letters. Sometime during 1942 he returned to Wisconsin and visited us at home in Durand. He drove his station wagon from Florida with some soldiers as passengers on his way to Madison, Wisconsin where he was stationed at Truax Field. It was a mystery to me how he managed to get enough gasoline to make that long drive from Florida because of gas rationing. While stationed at Truax Field Andy traded the station wagon and bought a better car, a small 1938 Chevy coupe.

Andy visited home regularly on weekends and always brought food packages with him from the Post Exchange. He couldn't have had very much

money since the soldiers in those days were paid very little something like $21 per month. Andy volunteered for overseas duty while at Truex Field and was sent to New Guinea. Everyone in Durand was proud of Andy since he had been one of the first from Durand to enlist. We always received letters from Andy while he was overseas from 1942 until the end of the war in 1945. On one occasion Andy had tried to visit Harry when they were both stationed in the Philippines but something got in the way and he missed seeing Harry. The failure to meet Harry must have been a big disappointment. The years he spent overseas were very difficult physically for Andy. When he arrived home after the war he was skin and bones and not at all well. He did not report his condition to army doctors for fear it would delay his getting home. We were expecting to hear in detail about his war experiences. Andy was very modest and it was very difficult to get him to tell us about the war. It was also very difficult for him to get started again in civilian life. The war had cost him 5 years. Andy lived at home in Durand for about one year after the war. He worked part time in the local Gamble store and the remainder of the time with Dad in the shop (without pay), mainly to help. The first thing he bought after he returned home was a new car. He was always generous with lending his car to the rest of us at home. The Nussberger family was large with 8 children and enjoyed playing cards (into early morning hours) and visiting at home. Often our sister Ruth and her family would spend Sundays at home and mother would prepare a family dinner (Fig. 15).

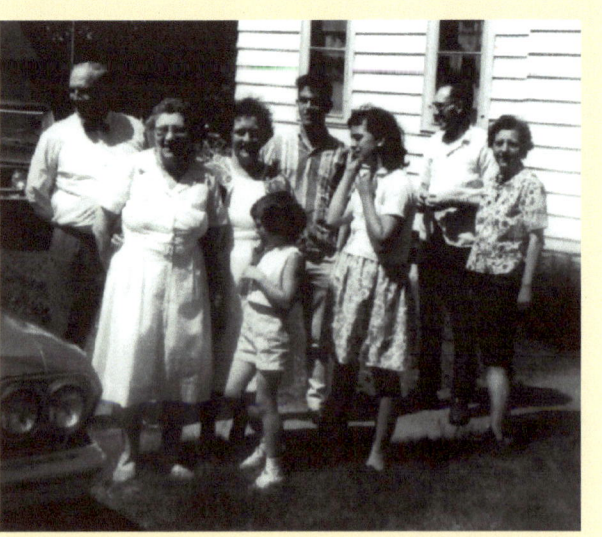

Figure 15. Nussberger family gathering for Sunday dinner (Kenneth, Mother, Ruth, Bobby, Joan, Andy, Adeline, and Virginia)

Adeline was living in Omaha, Nebraska and Adeline would visit us in Durand during the summer. Adeline would bring her two children (Corinne and Brendan) with her on these visits. Mark would stay in Omaha on the job (Fig. 16).

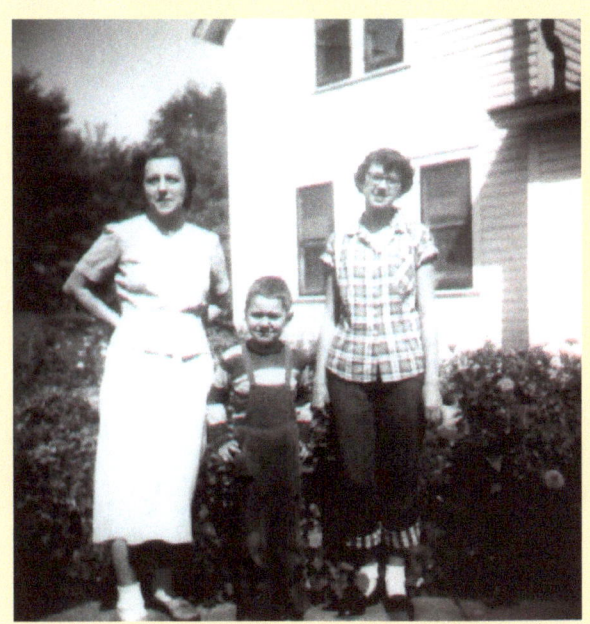

Figure 16. Adeline with Corrine and Brendan 1952

Nussberger children played together...

As children, Donald and Hubert played together (Fig. 17) while Andy and Ruth played together. Ruth was the outdoor type. Adeline wanted to stay indoors more and so Andy and Ruth would wind up playing outdoors together. In winter they would slide with their sleighs, down the old school hill at St. Mary's in Durand. St. Mary's school was not far from our home and that is where they went to school together. They would catch rides with some of the horse drawn sleighs that were in town. They would just hang on and get a free ride, then let go when they wanted to. Sundays they would walk uptown and buy candy. At that time you could get a lot of candy for 1 or 2 cents.

Christmas time at home...

At Christmas time Andy and Ruth would take candy canes and cookies from the back of the Christmas tree and go for a walk eating their treats. They had to sneak them as Mother wanted them left

on the tree until it was time to take the tree down. It was fun and Mother really didn't mind. One day Ruth was scrubbing the kitchen floor and Andy came through onto the wet floor. Ruth sort of whacked him on his pants pocket and he had eggs in the pocket. Andy cried, "Now you have broken my eggs". He had gotten the eggs from Grandpa Boehm. Grandpa and Grandma Boehm lived next door and Andy liked to bring something home from their house. Andy and Ruth would often climb the woodpile by the fence and jump over and pick some of Grandpa's plumbs. They had fun doing this and would rather do this than simply go over and ask for them.

Part 3. A Family Tragedy...
Mother away from home...

There was only two times that Mother left Durand for any extended time period. The first occurred during my sophomore year in high school. While mother was gone the upstairs caught fire and by the time Durand's volunteer fire department got the fire out it had destroyed the upstairs. Dad did the entire remodeling of the upstairs and I helped him clean up the mess. During a Sunday afternoon we were shoveling lath and plaster out an upstairs window onto a trailer parked beneath the window. Dad went down to move the trailer and I kept right on shoveling the plaster out of the window. He shouted to stop and looking out the window I saw him covered with plaster. Dad never scolded me. Of course there were rumors that a careless son who was trying to smoke coffee grounds caused this fire. Regardless the official cause of the fire was faulty wiring.

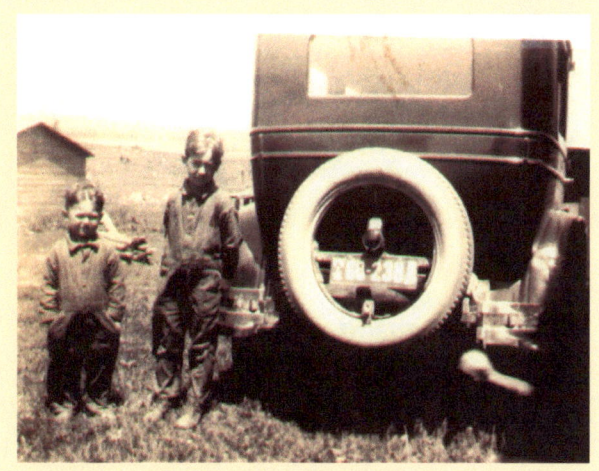

Figure 17. Donald and Hubert 1927

The second time mother left us alone was during my junior year in high school. This time the events were very sad and devastating to the entire family. Andy drove Mother to Omaha, Nebraska to visit Adeline and her family. On Saturday March 29, 1947, about 5 o'clock in the morning, Dad got a long distance telephone call informing him that there had been an early morning fire and that Hubert's wife Esther and their two small children, Judith, 2, and Richard, one year old, were dead (Figs. 18 and 19)

unsuccessful attempt to rescue the two children asleep in an adjoining room. Firemen found Esther's body near a rear door clutching the body of her young son and Judith was found in her crib wrapped in blankets. Hubert lost consciousness an hour before he died at 3:25 p.m. That very Saturday was the day that they were to move into a new home that they had recently purchased. Hubert and Esther were married October 28, 1944 in Milwaukee and the family is buried in Calvary Cemetery in Sheboygan, Wisconsin.

We drove to Sheboygan...

Dad, Ronald, and I drove to Sheboygan in the Studebaker but by the time we arrived Hubert was already dead. I drove the automobile since Dad did not like to drive. Dad had taught me to drive when I was only 13 years old. Dad believed that I would be able to get an emergency driver's license at 14 years. On my 14th birthday Dad left me at the sheriff's office with the Studebaker to take the driving test. The sheriff sent me home and said to come back at 16 as he watched me drive away.

Hubert loved to hunt and fish...

Hubert was the 4th oldest child and the second oldest boy (Fig. 20). He loved the outdoors and hunting and fishing (Fig. 21). Hubert convinced

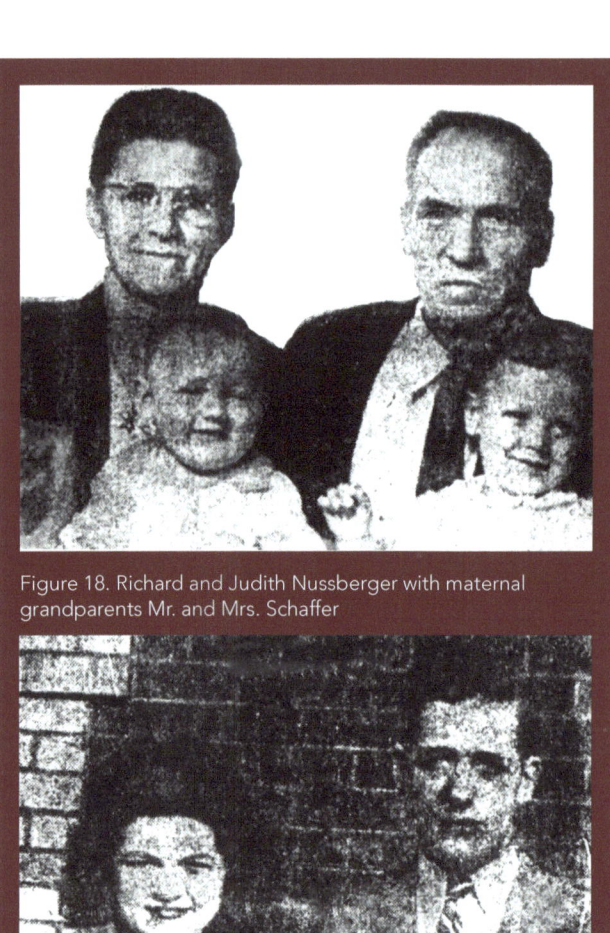

Figure 18. Richard and Judith Nussberger with maternal grandparents Mr. and Mrs. Schaffer

Figure 19. Esther Schaffer Nussbergaer and Hubert

Morning of the fire...

Hubert was in the hospital and not expected to live. Hubert had been driven from the home shortly before 4 a.m. when his pajamas caught fire. He and his wife groped their way through the smoke in an

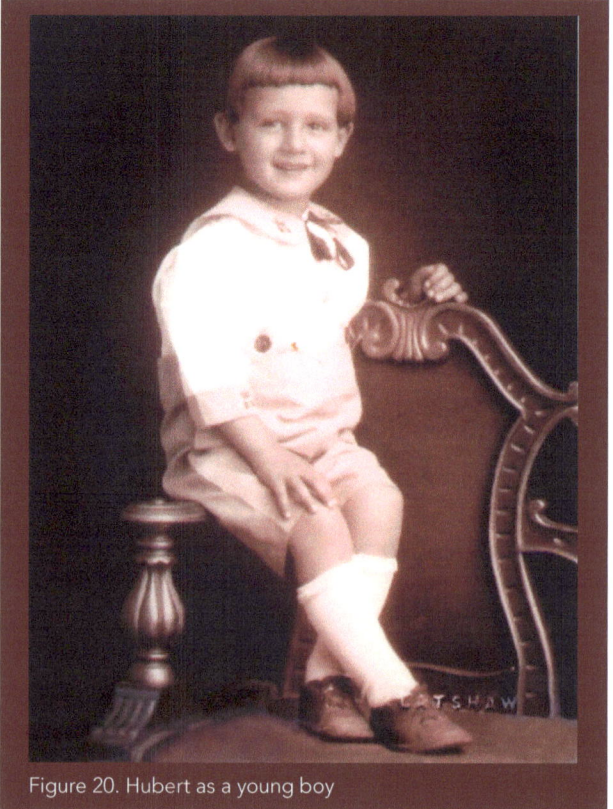

Figure 20. Hubert as a young boy

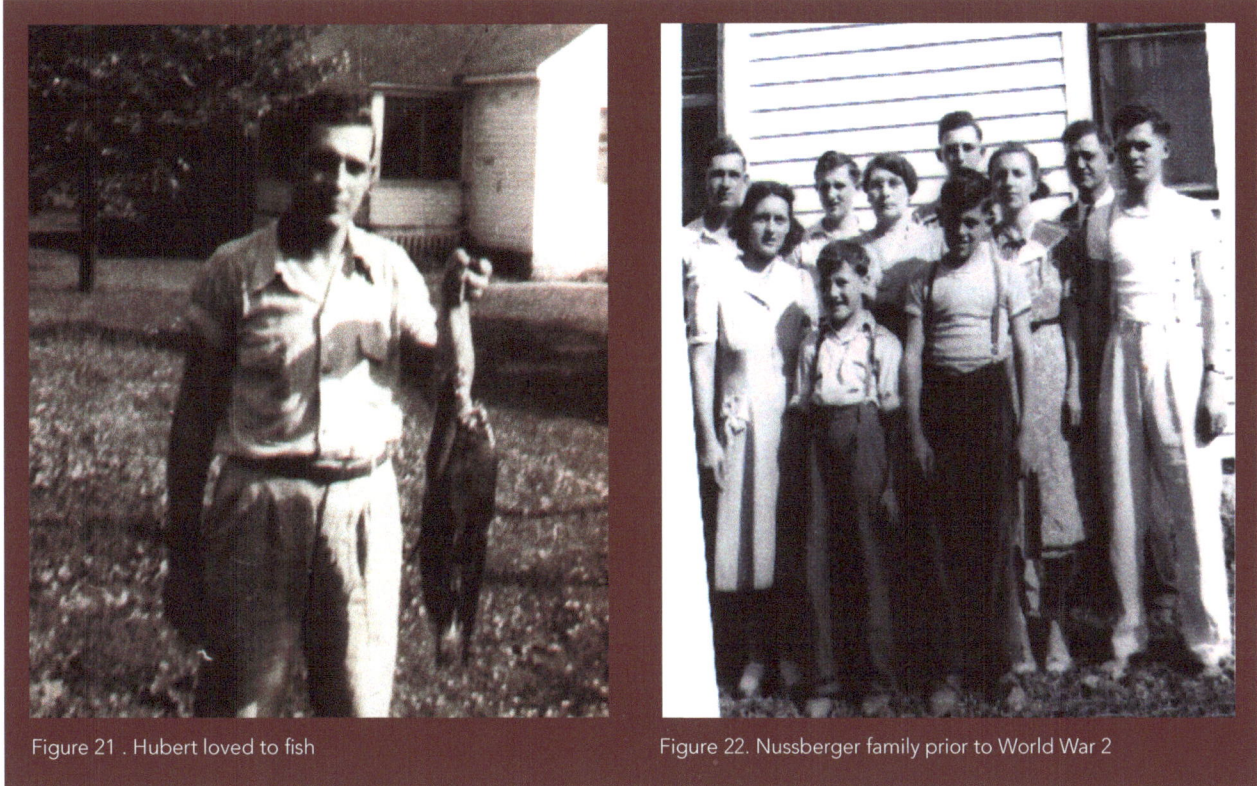

Figure 21 . Hubert loved to fish   Figure 22. Nussberger family prior to World War 2

Dad to buy an outboard motor boat and keep it on the Chippewa River. The motor was too powerful for the boat and Dad worried about Hubert using the boat. One summer Dad had the motor in a repair shop for the entire summer on an excuse that it needed work. Mother told me that Dad only kept the motor in the repair shop because he was worried about it being too powerful for the boat. Hubert did not know about Dad's concern. In later years, Dad let me use the boat but without the motor. It was a 16-foot boat and rowing it gave me plenty of exercise.

Part 4. *Arthur's Story*

Growing up in a small town ...

Our family was large, 2 girls and 6 boys (Fig. 22), each of us took care of our own possessions. Dad gave each of us a weekly allowance and we bought our own things with the money.

Dad and mother set the example ...

Dad was hard working and honest, his word was his bond and the people of Durand knew and respected him. All of our groceries were ordered over the telephone and delivered to our house. Mother would make a list and telephone in the order. At the end of the month, Dad would visit the grocer and pay the monthly bill. There wasn't a single person in town that

did not trust him. On one occasion he sold the lot next to the family home and made a handshake agreement that if either party backed out of the deal that party would pay a $500 penalty fee. Mother objected to the sale and Dad paid the $500 penalty. The example of hard work and honesty set by both parents taught us children to work hard and persevere.

Peanut butter episode ...

One very early experience that I remember was the "peanut butter" episode. While very young, about the age of 5, I had a huge jar of peanut butter that was mine alone. I don't remember how I got the peanut butter but I do recall hiding it in my clothes closet. At mealtime I would sneak the jar out of the closet when no one was looking and bring it out to the kitchen table. One morning I was in a hurry and dropped the jar on the floor and it broke wide open. The peanut butter was all over the floor and I was sick. I never could afford enough money to buy myself another jar of peanut butter.

Ski splitting ...

Something like the peanut butter thing happened with my first pair of skis. The skis were children's skis and I was about six years old. Behind St. Mary's (our school) there was a large hill and in the winter the kids would ski down the hill. The older boys

15

built a high jump at the foot of the hill and one day I decided to go over that jump. It took a lot of nerve but coming down that hill was exciting and over the jump I went. I landed on my feet but when my skis hit the ground one of the skis split down the middle. I might have become a great ski person if the skis hadn't split or if I would have been able to buy myself another pair of skis.

Childhood accidents ...

Growing up I had a number of accidents. Before I was 5, Dad often took me with him in the car on Sundays to his shop. Mother told me that twice I fell out of the car during these drives to the shop. Once I dove off the headboard of my bed and into the mattress. I remember standing on the headboard and debating about diving head long into the bed like it was water. I jumped head first into the mattress. The most serious accident I had as a child was at the age of 5 years in a farm accident. Mother was visiting a cousin on a farm at the edge of Durand. Harry and I were riding on the platform of a stone crusher being pulled by a team of horses. Someone shouted to jump off and I jumped in the wrong direction and in front of the stone crusher instead of behind it. I was taken home unconscious and remember waking up in our living room with Dr. Scott (our family doctor) bending over me. Mother, Dad, and Frank Schuh, the driver of the horses, were in the background and looked worried. In a few minutes I fell back into unconsciousness. For several weeks I was in bed recovering or walking around with an arm in a sling and getting lots of attention. I don't know if these accidents had anything to do with my mother's pre birth activity. Dr. Scott, our family doctor, advised mother to drink beer during her pregnancy. Each afternoon mother would wait in the car while dad went into the tavern with a honey pail. Dad would bring the pail out to mother and she would drink the beer. I sometimes wondered if the beer had anything to do with my many accidents as a child.

Making coffee the hard way...

We lived a couple of houses from the Chippewa River bank. Below our house there was a creek that fed into the river. It came down from the hills behind St. Mary's school. One afternoon I went down to the river by the creek with two neighbor friends and we brewed some coffee in an open fire. I got the grounds from mother's kitchen and when the water started boiling we realized that there was no way to get the pan out of the fire. One of the

boys said that he knew how to remove the pan. We watched as he went back a distance and ran over the fire kicking the pan out of the fire, and he was one of the smarter boys in school. Looking over the spilled coffee I remember wondering, **"Should I be playing with such a dumbbell?"**

Smoking as a child ...

Smoking was popular and most boys tried it at a young age. I remember smoking corn silk using a home made corncob pipe. Once I even tried coffee grounds but it made me sick. When we had the money we bought Marvel cigarettes at ten cents a pack and sat up in the neighbor's hayloft and smoked away. One of my neighbor friends had a barn at the back of their property and we would climb up into the hayloft and smoke. We kept our cigarettes hidden in the loft. I imagine if the barn had caught fire we would have had to admit our part in it (Figs. 23).

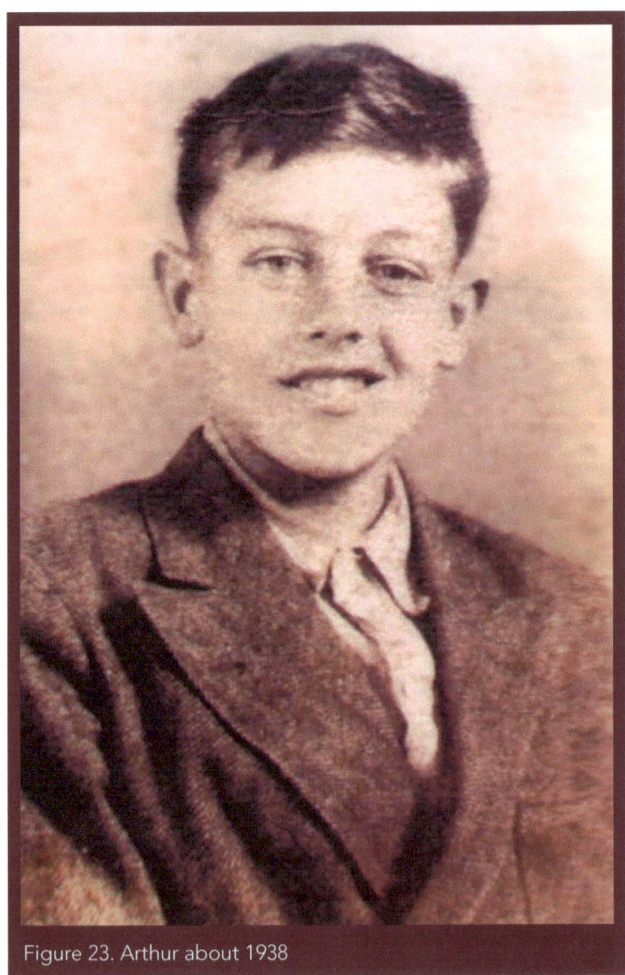

Figure 23. Arthur about 1938

16

Mother's family lived in Halder, Wisconsin and in the summertime the folks often drove the 100 miles to visit the Boehm families. The older boys had a small cigarette-rolling machine. I knew where they hid it and sometimes when the folks left and we were home alone I would get the machine and roll my own cigarettes. Oddly enough, even though I started smoking very young, I never got addicted to smoking and in later years easily quit smoking, without pain.

Plumb fights in the back yard...

Grandpa Boehm lived next door and had an orchard of plum trees. Each spring we made slingshots and had plumb fights around our house. We would get stung a few times but no one got hurt. We also enjoyed playing fort and running around the neighbor's house. Unfortunately we often ran in opposite directions and we had many a collision. We also enjoyed jumping off the neighbor's shed. We could also be very mischievous. I remember once locking a neighbor kid in our garage with the intention of giving him a beating. The scared kid cried and "pissed" his pants and was afraid that his mother would punish him. We felt sorry for him and let him out of the garage (Fig. 24).

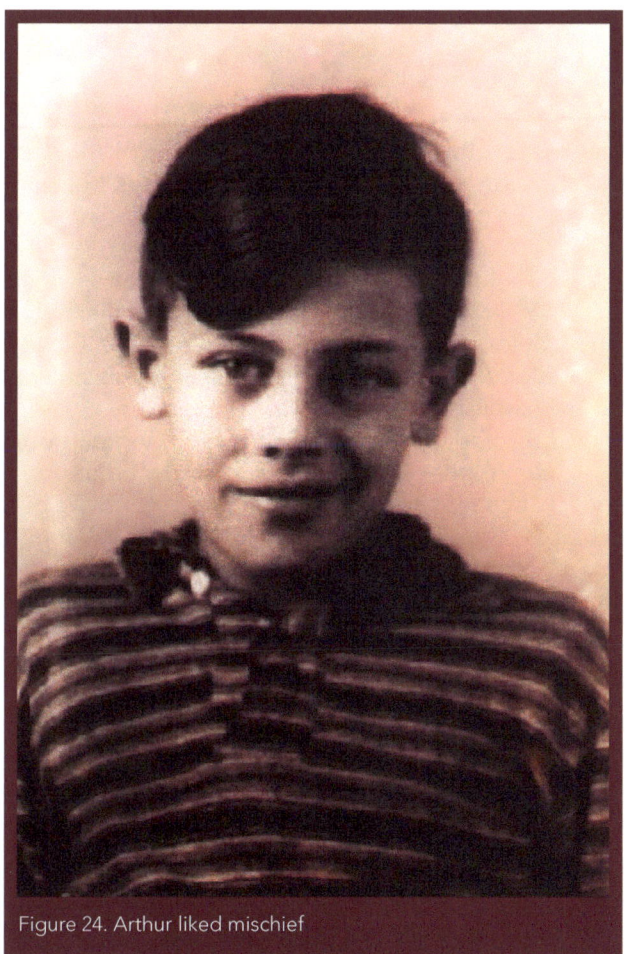

Figure 24. Arthur liked mischief

Bicycle wish ...

When I was very young I remember wanting a bicycle and going to the shop looking for dad to surprise me with a bike. After waiting years patiently for the bicycle, I finally got one for $5 and it was the thrill of my youth. Later I was able to buy a smart looking bike for $25. After using the bike for a number of years I sold it to a boy for the price I paid. He took the bike promising to pay me later. After a few weeks I found out that he didn't have any money to pay me and I repossessed the bike.

Outdoor fun ...

We spent most of our free time outdoors. We would set lines out overnight along the riverbank to catch fish. Sometimes we would get down to the river early and mess around with some of the other fishermen's lines. At the mouth of the creek that fed into the river there were carp and catfish that fed from the creek. One summer I caught a large carp and sold it to a truck driver for 50 cents. He was delivering milk to the old brewery that had been converted into a casein plant to make plastics. The driver would park in front of our house waiting his turn to unload. Each day I would sell him a large carp and he would take the carp home and smoke it for food to feed his family.

Christmas time ...

Christmas time was fun. Each of the kids got one present. There were Christmas apples in the cellar and we got to mail order our Christmas candy orders. The candy would come a few weeks later and we would hoard them away. The cellar also contained some dandy lion wine that Grandpa Boehm was fond of making. I can remember one Christmas Eve walking to attend Midnight Mass and it was snowing – a truly white Christmas.

Arthur raises chickens ...

Shortly after recovering from the stone crusher accident Dad bought several dozen chicks for me to raise. He built a chicken coupe using six old doors and we added a heater for the chicks, Dad bought the feed and I tended to the chicks. Eventually the chicks out grew there make shift coupe and Dad gave me use of the garage for their shelter. For several years I raised the chickens and they turned into hens. I collected the eggs and sold them to a local store. I would keep tract of each hen and how many eggs it laid. The eggs would accumulate and after a few dozen were collected I would wash them and pack them into a crate and sell the eggs to the local food store. Needless to say, it took a long time to get together enough eggs for marketing and I now wonder how fresh those eggs really were. I never got a complaint. I would spend a lot of time in the garage with my chickens. I had a bee bee gun and enjoyed shooting flies off the wall or off the screen door. One day Ron showed up at the screen door just as I was shooting the gun. He got hit above the eye and Mother demanded that I get rid of the gun. I hid it inside the wallboards of the garage and maybe it is still there?

Playing in the house ...

We had fun inside the house. Often Adeline and Mark would visit for the weekend. After Adeline married, she and Mark settled in Halder, Wisconsin living in Mark's family home. We were always excited for their visit since Mark loved to play with us kids. We often played inside tossing the ball to each other. Growing up we loved to play cards. Mark introduced us to a German game called shoffskoff. We played the game for hours, sometimes until 2 or 3 in the morning. The game was played for change and I usually won spending money. At midnight we would stop for a sandwich and refreshments.

Helping mother ...

The family always ate in the kitchen (Fig. 25). We had a large round table that was big enough to seat the entire family. The only time that I can remember eating in the living room was at Adeline's wedding reception dinner. One day we were misbehaving and mother was chasing us around the kitchen table with a flyswatter in hand. We heard something at the door and looking in the glass at the top of the door was Uncle Henry. I remember how embarrassed mother was. We did help mother with the canning. In the summer she canned strawberries and peaches. I remember picking over strawberries most of the morning getting the berries ready for canning.

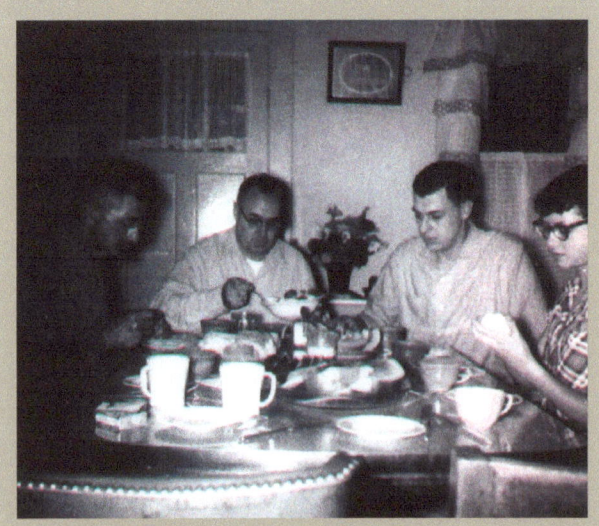

Figure 25. Eating in the kitchen

School at St. Mary's...

We all attended St. Mary's school from Grades 1 through the 10th. Our last two years were spent in Durand High School. St. Mary's was located on Prospect Street within easy walking distance from home (Fig. 26). I got in trouble early in school. I remember getting kicked out of our first grade Christmas play. I went up to the shop and Hubert was working there. One of the first graders came by and started telling Hubert that I got kicked out of the play.

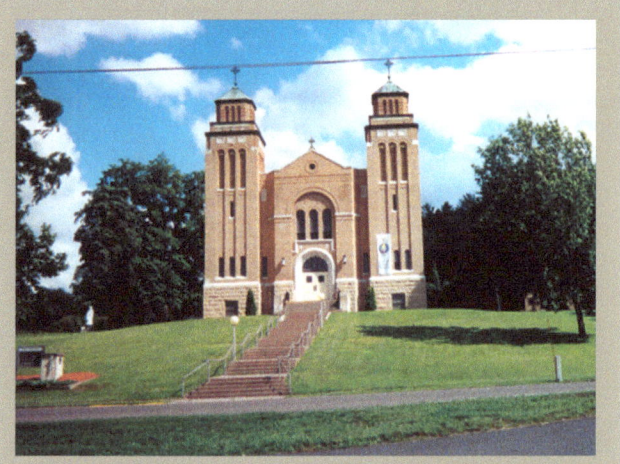

Figure 26. St. Mary's church

He insisted that I had been chased out of the play. Hubert didn't believe him and threatened to beat him up and the boy ran away. During confirmation practice Fr. Kellenhoffer chased me and another boy out of the church for talking during practice. I was really worried that mother would find out. She loved Fr. Kellenhoffer and would have been mortified. Father K sent for us a couple of days later to meet with him in his office. To my surprise and amazement he was very pleasant and reassured us that it wasn't a big thing and only that he felt it necessary to keep order. Mother never found out about it. Coming home from school we had to cross Prospect Street, a major highway through town. One after noon crossing the highway I ran into the side of a car. I remember the driver stopping and chasing after me to see if I was all right. Fortunately no harm was done and I continued on my way home. The driver looked more frightened than I felt.

The family car ...

At the age of 9 years, I experienced for the first time being afraid and thinking I am in trouble with Dad. The family car was a 1937 Studebaker sedan and it was kept in the garage. I learned how to back it up, by pulling on the starter on the dashboard. One day while backing the car it hit the side of the garage and damaged the front door. Dad always came home for lunch and I hid behind a neighbor's tree in fear of being punished. To my surprise nothing ever happened about the car accident and it is doubtful that Dad ever found out. The car was bought from Hubbard's Studebaker garage. In 1937 Hubbard's didn't have the money to get the car from the factory and Dad advanced Mr. Hubbard the $1100 needed. Andy Jr. went to South Bend, Indiana and picked up the car at the factory and drove it home. The car was wrecked twice and each time rebuilt, once in 1938 and a second time in 1939. Dad never blamed the boys for the accidents but did resolve that he would never buy a new car again. The Studebaker got lots of use. In the spring of 1938 Adeline was teaching in a rural school several miles outside Durand and each day Hubert would drive her to and from school.

Driving at 13 ...

Dad taught me to drive at 13 years. Mother didn't drive and the older boys had all left home. Dad thought I would be given a driver's license at 14 years. On my 14th birthday, we drove to the sheriff's office and dad left me with the car and walked back to his shop. Sheriff Saline came out to the car and talked to me at the curbside. He informed me that I had to wait until I was 16 years old to take the test. I got into the car and drove away with the sheriff standing on the sidewalk. Dad didn't like to drive on the highway and I did all the family driving. One pleasant memory was driving our St. Mary's nuns around the school playground. The nuns got into our 1937 Studebaker and were absolutely delighted to ride in a car even though it was only across the playground. My 5th grade teacher was one of the nuns. She was the principal of St. Mary's and I always thought that she didn't like me. She was very strict and it surprised me that she was so delighted to be riding in our old Studebaker. Two of my favorite teachers were my fourth grade and ten grade teachers. The fourth grade teacher was a novice (very young and hadn't yet taken her final vows) and offered me an "A" if I would please stop talking to the 3rd grade girl sitting next to me. My 10th grade teacher showed that she liked me and really motivated me to get serious about studies. Later when I was teaching high school in Milwaukee, one Saturday afternoon I drove the nuns from our high school to their mother convent home. We used the school bus and they filled the bus. The nuns all wore habits and were most appreciative of the smallest favor. The trip reminded me of the St. Mary's nuns riding across the playground. The nuns were wonderful women and it was heart warming to help them in a small way. On one occasion Uncle I.G.

visited us and stayed overnight. The next morning I drove him to a neighboring town to catch the bus. He gave me $5 and I bought the most expensive fishing lure I could find. I fished with it on Thompson's lake and caught the biggest fish I ever saw. But in pulling in the fish the line broke and I lost the fish and the lure. I never could afford such an expensive lure again.

Blackie our dog ...

One summer Andy brought home a stray cocker spaniel. He found the dog abandoned in a quarry and the dog became a family pet. It was black and we named him blackie. He was both an indoor and outdoor dog but was afraid of the water. He wasn't afraid of other dogs and usually chased them away. He would sleep on the cellar trap door and eat scraps from the table.

Firecrackers on the 4th of July ...

As I got older, I spent one summer working in the pop factory across from the shop. I was paid 50 cents a half day and worked washing pop bottles and labeling the larger bottles. I also went with the delivery truck and helped unload the cases of pop to the local taverns. In the evenings we enjoyed going to the movies. The theatre was at the end of Main Street and I would either walk to the theatre or ride my bike. Each Fourth of July we would buy firecrackers and blow up tin cans or throw the lighted firecrackers out of our bedroom window. One fourth of July I remember getting home late from the movies and seeing our neighbor sleeping by the window in his living room. I dropped a firecracker outside his window and watched him jump. Our neighbor was an elderly man and liked to sport a cane. He was the janitor at St. Mary's and liked to tell the story that he once threatened Fr. Kellenhofer with standing in the back of the church and pounding his cane on the floor if the sermon was too long. Fr. Kellenhofer told him that if he ever did that then he would be chased out of the church, cane and all.

Hunting and fishing ...

Thompson Lake was located a couple of miles out of town on the highway to Minneapolis. The lake was on both sides of the road with a bridge spanning a channel of the lake. In the summer we would bicycle to the lake and craw under the viaduct and sit at the edge of the concrete dangling our legs over the water and kid each other. One afternoon, one of the boys mentioned that the water below us was 30 feet deep. It took a moment to sink in as we looked down into the water, then there was a sudden mad scramble to get out from under the bridge. That was my last time sitting under the bridge.

Dad let me use Hubert's boat but without the motor. I oared it out onto the Chippewa River and spent many happy hours on the river. I don't remember ever catching any fish but it didn't matter. One spring we found a large canoe floating down the Chippewa River. The river always peaked during the spring thaw and somehow the canoe must have gotten free from its mooring. The canoe replaced Hubert's boat and was quite an improvement since it was much easier to row and easier to maneuver on the river. In the fall I spent many happy hours walking down the railroad tracks chasing quail. I had an old 22 gauge single shot rifle and I don't remember hitting anything but it didn't matter.

Dr. Scott our family doctor...

We did some gardening in the summer. We always planted a field of potatoes. Dad took pride in the potato patch and we helped out by digging up the potatoes in the fall. We also grew poppies and some table vegetables. One summer I worked in the garden and developed a terrible infection in my left foot. Dr. Scott came to the house every day and pealed away the scab and poured disinfectant on the foot. It really smarted. He would bandage the foot and I would hop around on one foot. Just before school started I remember Dr. Scott saying it is time to heal up the foot so I could go back to school. Dr. Scott did exactly that and within days the foot was healed. Dr. Scott owned a farm about 30 minutes out of town. He bought it for his son who was in the army during the Second World War. There was no one living on the farm and Dr. Scott and myself would drive out there in the evening. He said it was a way for him to relax. We would put up fences and feed the little pigs he was raising. He was thinking about getting a cow but neither of us knew how to milk a cow. They would have to be fed and cared for. Later his daughter in law moved onto the farm and we gradually shortened the visits.

National Radio Institute course...

Dad enjoyed conversation but more as a listener than as a talker. He would listen for hours to Hubert telling about his work as a welder working in Milwaukee and at other times listening to Kenneth (Ruth's husband) talk about his teaching experiences, and still other times to I.G. (mother's oldest brother) telling stories about the insurance business. Dad was very interested in technical subjects and particularly liked electronics. During my sophomore year in high school, Dad bought me a 36-month home correspondence course from the National Radio Institute to learn how to repair radios. This course consisted of weekly lessons and a monthly experiment package to build test equipment and the various stages of a superheteordyne radio. My bedroom was filled with spare radio parts and old radios. I remember taking high school physics and looking at the last half of the text book that was devoted to electricity. I anxiously waited for the teacher to get to that part of the book but it never happened. During the winter months I spent many Sunday afternoons with Dad in the living room discussing the National Radio Institute lessons and the technical details of building and repairing radios. The National Radio Institute promised that I could retake the course at any time – I wonder what they would say if I applied to retake the course? Dad seldom criticized or complained. One evening in 1945 Dad went upstairs to watch me work on a radio experiment. A heated soldering iron had been left on the chair and Dad accidentally sat on it. After a minute or so we both started to smell smoldering corduroy pants. Dad left in a hurry but never complained or scolded about it. The next morning Mother told me that Dad had a very severe burn on his backside.

Attending college ...

In 1948 Dad wanted me to become a radio repairman and go into business with him using part of the shop building. I was enrolled into a technical school in Chicago (Coyne Electrical Institute) to complete a course to learn electronics and radio repair. The idea of going to Chicago was appealing but a radio repairman was not my idea of a vocation. I wanted to go to college and become an engineer and waited until the last possible minute to talk to Dad about wanting to change plans. During our discussion Dad never complained even though he was disappointed. Dad agreed that I would attend Stout Institute (now a campus of the University of Wisconsin) located in Menomonee, Wisconsin, live at home (to save money) and drive the 22 miles to attend classes. At the time, driving that far everyday was nearly unthinkable since the roads were county roads and the winter weather often made them nearly impossible to travel. Dad agreed to buy a 1942 Studebaker from Hubbard's garage and advance me an allowance of $10 each week for expenses. After a few weeks in school I learned to live on less than $10 and one Saturday I handed back $5 and said, "I can get by on $5 a week"! Dad's expression was surprise and from that day on he enthusiastically backed me to obtain a college degree. Giving back $5 a week convinced Dad that I was sincere in wanting an education and that it would be worth the sacrifice.

Living in Milwaukee ...

After graduating from college in June of 1952 (Fig. 27), I accepted a job to teach Industrial Arts in a Milwaukee Catholic high school. To live in Milwaukee I needed a car and Dad agreed to advance the money needed to buy my first car. He sent me to Minneapolis with $800 cash and instructions not to spend more that $600 and to trade in the old 1937 Studebaker. I went from used car lot to used car lot and couldn't find a car that I liked within the $600 limit. One car that I liked and wanted to buy was a 1947 Pontiac, but the price was $750. I gave up the search and late that afternoon started back home to Durand. At the outskirts of Minneapolis I changed my mind and decided to go back and buy the Pontiac and face Dad. I paid $750 in cash and the salesman, absolutely dumfounded, gave me a lecture on the dangers in the city of carrying such a large amount of cash. When I got home, to my complete surprise, Dad was delighted and mentioned that he would have been deeply disappointed if I had returned driving the old 1937 Studebaker.

Moving to California ...

In 1956 I accepted a job as a design engineer with North American Aviation and moved to California. I married Rose Ann in 1963 and settled in Buena Park, California where we raised three children, Gregory, Julie, and Suzanne. In 1975 the family moved from Buena Park to Riverside, California. We still live in Riverside. Gregory lives in Tucson, Arizona and is the father of three children; Julie lives in Moreno Valley California raising 3 children and Suzanne in Huntsville, Alabama raising five children. Grandpa Arthur has written a "Silly" book describing the antiques of 11 grand children. Rose Ann was always interested in the arts and has completed some very good art pieces including marble sculpturing, bronze pieces, and paintings. For several years she participated in tap dancing exhibits with a team including Julie and Suzanne (Fig. 28). Rose Ann's team would perform dance recitals for local benefits. Rose Ann is famous around Riverside for her artwork having owned and operated her own art gallery, the Riverside Gallery of

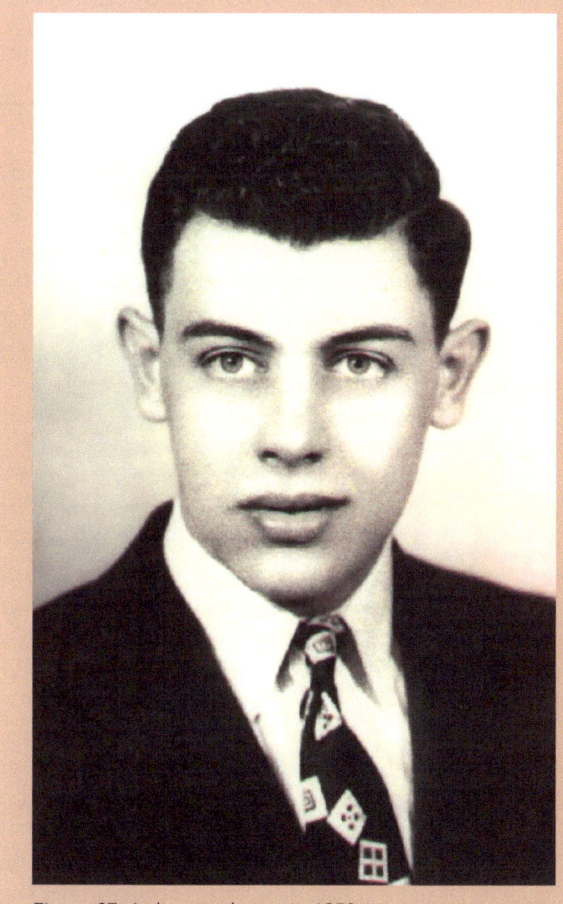

Figure 27. Arthur graduates in 1952

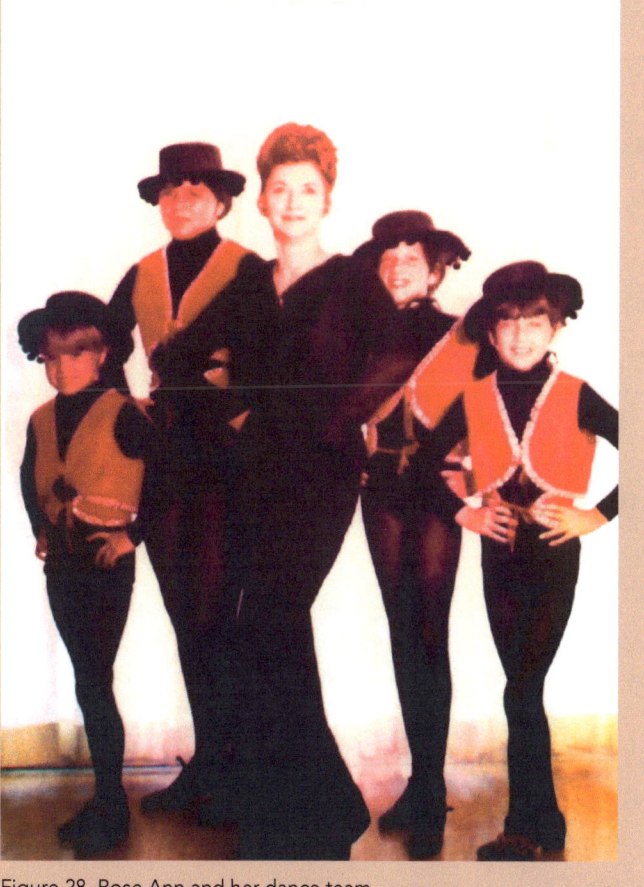

Figure 28. Rose Ann and her dance team

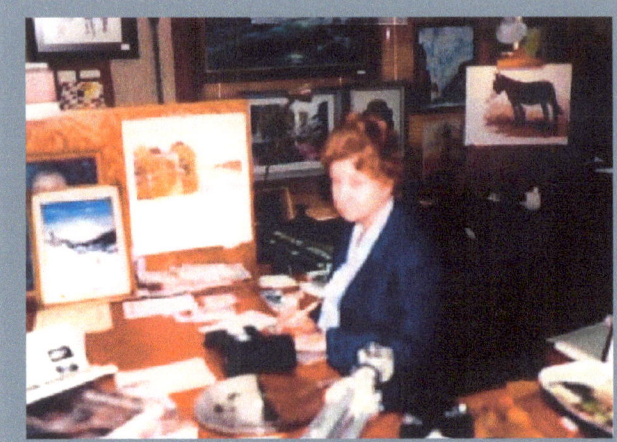

Figure 29. Rose Ann and the Riverside Gallery of Arts

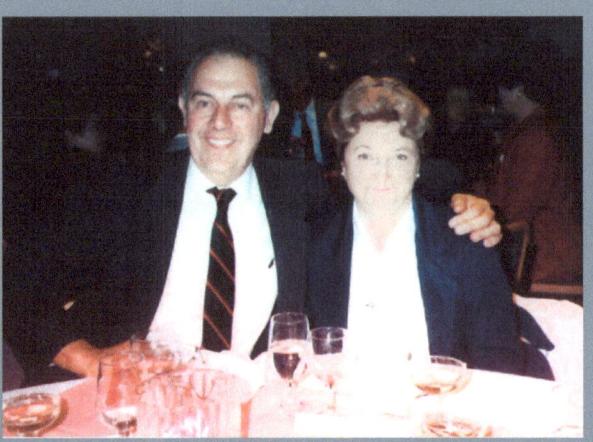

Figure 31 . Arthur and Rose Ann enjoy living in California 1990.

Arts (Fig. 29). In the 1960's and 1970's we had many visits from Adeline and Andy (Fig. 30). It was always a pleasure to visit with members of the family. Living in California isolated us from the family in Wisconsin (Fig. 31). We did manage several automobile trips back to Wisconsin but they were few and far between. I traveled a great deal as part of my job. Often these trips gave me a chance to stop over in Chicago on a weekend and visit Harry and Alice.

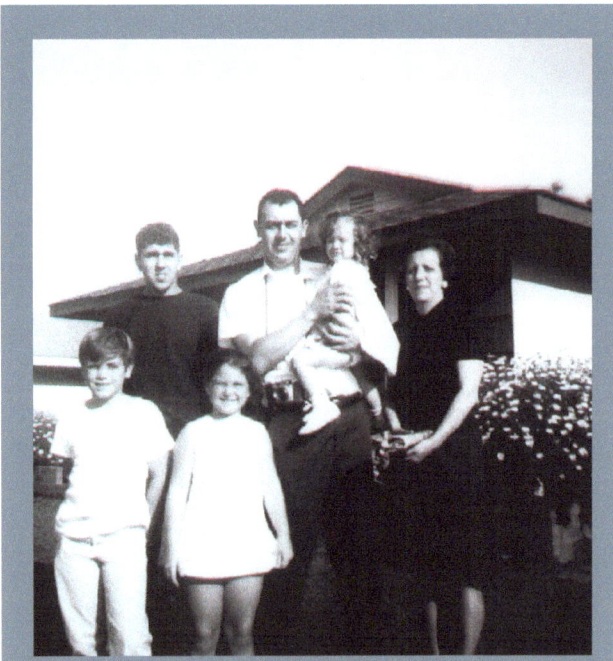

Figure 30. Adeline visits in California

I continued my education in California and graduated from California State University at Los Angeles with a Bachelor of Science degree in Engineering (1958) and from the University of Southern California with a Master of Science degree in Mechanical Engineering (1967) At one time in the nuclear engineering department. My specialty at work was designing electrical power systems for space applications and it looked like we would be using nuclear systems in space. I had completed my course work and about to start a thesis program when I realized that the space program would not go nuclear because of nuclear safety issues. Public opinion on nuclear changed dramatically in the mid 1960's. While I was at UCLA, as a student, it was common for us to conduct experiments using the nuclear reactor located in the basement of the engineering building. The reactor has long since been removed and conducting such experiments today would be unthinkable.

Mother and Dad provided examples of dedication and hard work that motivated us. I credit my success to the work ethics instilled by our parents. During 30 years at Rockwell's Space Division I achieved key engineering positions in the design and development of the Apollo Command and Service Module, Saturn II booster stage, Space Shuttle Orbiter, International Space Station and Global Positioning Satellite (GPS). I also participated as Project Engineer in preliminary design of many of our nations planned advanced space systems. In 1982 I was honored as Rockwell's nomination for engineer of the year and in 1985 received Rockwell's highest award for excellence, the Presidents Award. As a member of a team working in the space program I experienced many of its successes and anxieties as man attempted to conquest space. Dad would have appreciated the magnitude and importance of our nation's space program and would have looked forward to the future with people working in space in a permanently manned earth orbital laboratory and space manufacturing facility. Dad believed in the future and often talked about the day when we would have space exploration. His favorite vision was looking forward to the day when we would have an automobile-airplane that combined traveling on the highway or flying like a plane.

Part 5. *Arthur's Legacy...*

The Grandchildren ...

Rose Ann and myself still live in California. Our three children live in various parts of the country: Gregory lives in Arizona, Julie in California, and Suzanne in Alabama (Fig. 32). The children were taught love of God, country and family. These values are now being taught to our grandchildren. Each grandchild provides a unique pleasure to the family. Everyday events are often funny and revealing.

There are 11 grandchildren. They were all involved in silly antics in growing up.

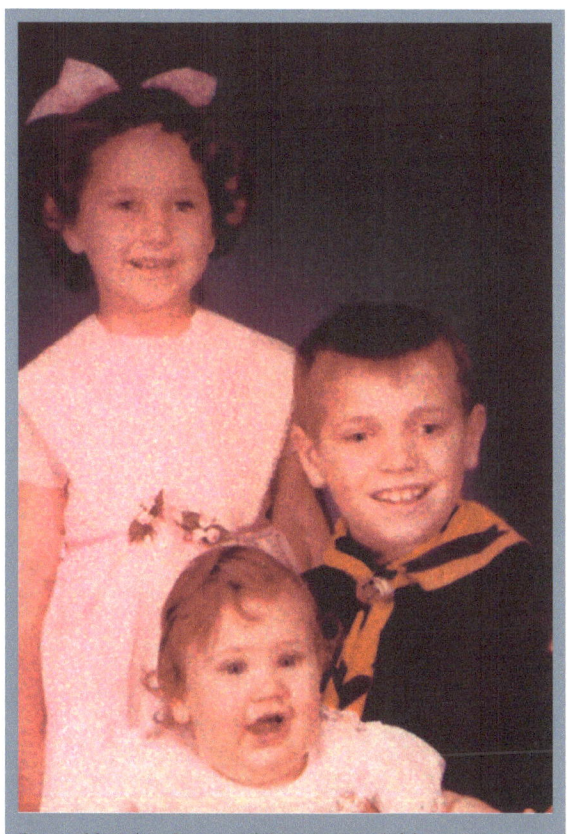

Figure 32. Julie, Greg, and Suzanne as children

Gregory's children...

The oldest grandchild is Kathleen (Gregory's) and she is in college (Fig. 33). Kathleen is remembered as a very observant child. When she was very young Grandma and Grandpa helped take care of her and on one occasion took her to the ball game. A neighbor couple drove us to Anaheim for an Angel baseball game. We were in the back seat and Kathleen wanted to know where she would sit at the game? She was told that she would sit next to Grandma and Grandpa.

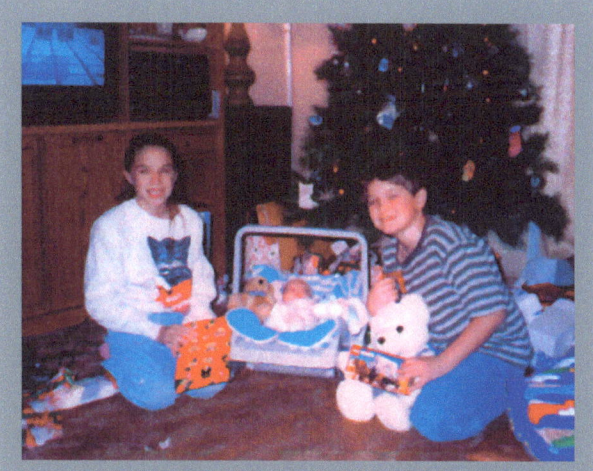

Figure 33. Kathleen and Gregory Jr. enjoying Christmas

not her father. Kathleen had trouble pronouncing l's and Grandpa liked to tease her. Grandpa made up a restaurant named Larry Logan's. Kathleen got irritated. Several weeks later Grandpa asked Kathleen which restaurant she wanted to go to? Kathleen said, "Any restaurant but Larry Logan's", Kathleen had mastered the l's. Gregory (Jay) is Greg's second child. He recently graduated from high school in Tucson, Arizona and loves to play football. Gregory settled arguments by saying, "I'm happy for you!" or he would say, "I'm sorry you feel that way". Greg's youngest is Dana (Fig. 34). She is being home schooled by her mother and is doing fantastically.

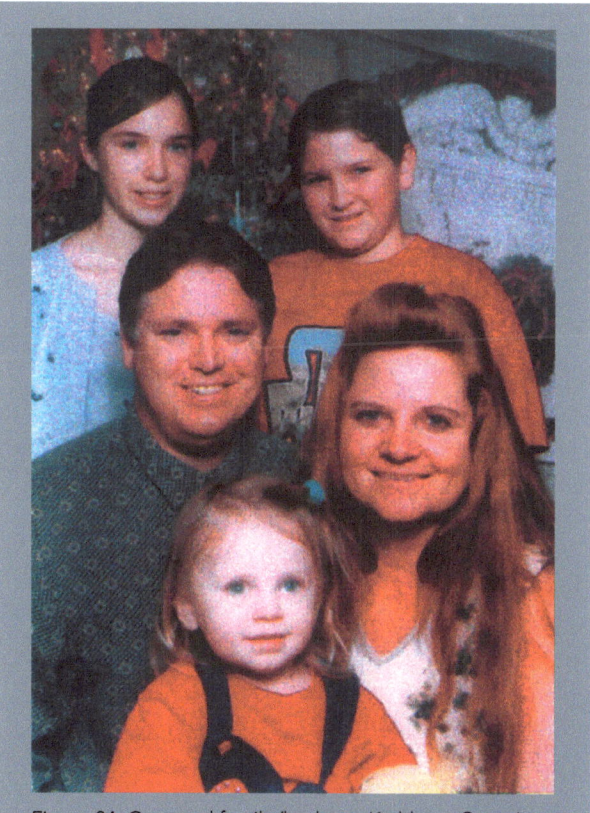

Figure 34. Greg and family (back row Kathleen, Greg Jr.; middle row Greg. Sir, Diana; and front row Dana)

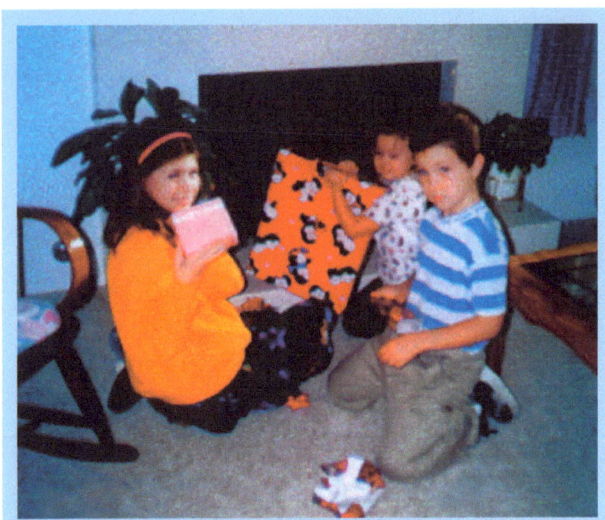
Figure 35. Nicole, Matthew, and Michelle

after me, but I shaped up1". Grandpa was taking Matthew and Nicole home from school and they were arguing and shouting at each other. Grandpa scolded them for being so rude. Matthew looked at Grandpa and said, "That is the way we like to talk to each other, do you have a problem with that?"

Michelle is Julie's baby and she is doing very well at St. Francis elementary school (Fig. 36). She is on the honor role and was selected student of the month for May. When Michelle was very young she loved Elvis. When she was three years old she loved to listen and dance to Elvis' music. One of Michelle's favorite movies was "Elvis on Tour". One day Michelle was enjoying an Elvis tune until the station changed to another singer. She was disappointed and complained, "That's not Elvis, its crap!" One day grandpa was baby sitting Michelle. She saw a grasshopper in the bathroom and told Grandpa about it. Grandpa called it a darn grasshopper and Michelle said, "don't use that word, that's the f word!" Grandpa was arguing with Grandma and Michelle knows that Grandma is always right. She asked Grandma, "Grandma why don't you just smack Grandpa?" Grandpa's dog was named BeBe and Michelle loved BeBe (Fig. 37). One day BeBe was cleaning herself and Michelle told Grandpa not to watch, BeBe needs privacy, "She is grooming herself!" Grandpa once asked Michelle what she thinks of Grandma? Michelle said, "I adore her!"

Julie's children...

Julie has three children (Fig. 35). The oldest is Nicole and she recently graduated from Notre Dame high school in Riverside, California. She earned a letter in swimming and is currently planning on becoming a registered nurse. During Nicole's grade school years Grandpa often tutored her in studies during her summer vacation. Grandpa said, "we will concentrate on Nicole this summer and Matthew next summer". Matthew is Julie's next oldest and he is currently enrolled in Notre Dame high school. Matthew loves chess and computer games. One day Matthew got into trouble and Grandpa corrected

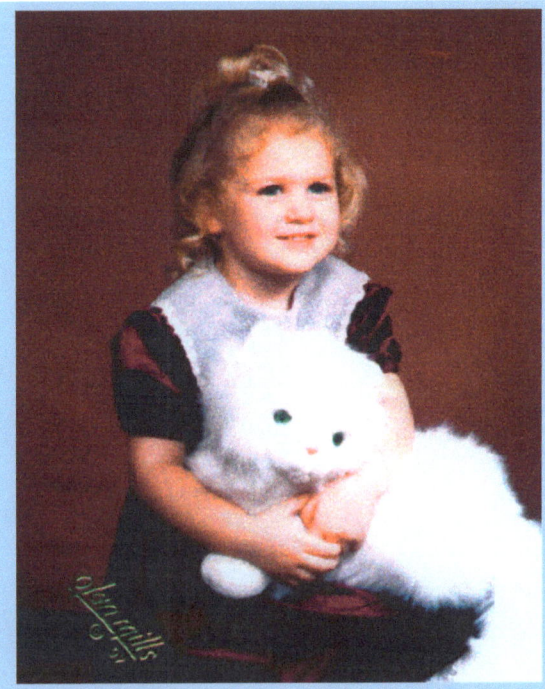
Figure 36. Michelle is Julie's youngest

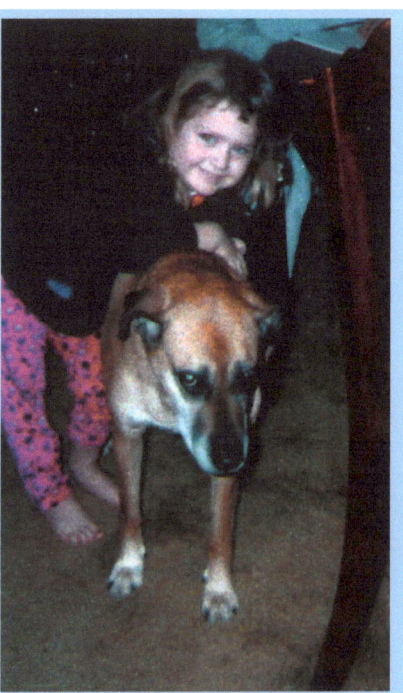
Figure 37. BeBe and Michelle

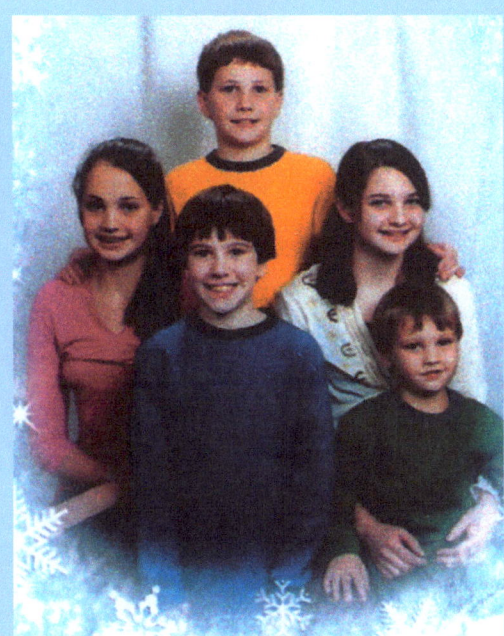

Figure 38. Suzanne's 5 children (back row Eric; middle row Alexis. Sammy, Baylee; front row. Luke)

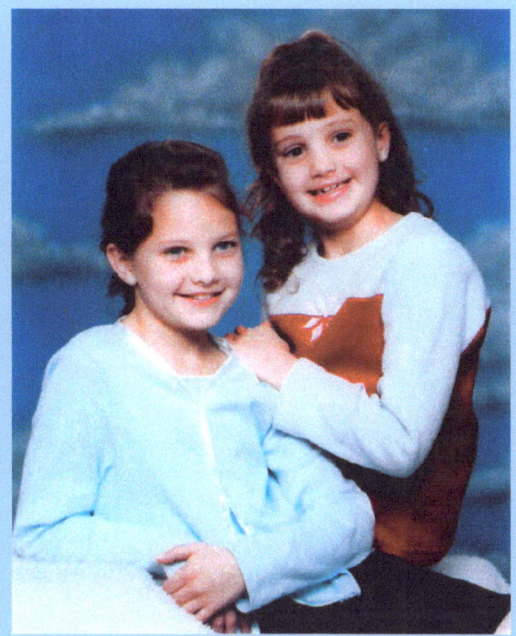

Figure 39 Baylee and Alexis

Suzanne's children...

Suzanne has five children (Fig. 38). We visit her as often as we can. Baylee is the oldest and she attends High School. Baylee is a cheerleader. Her brother Eric plays quarterback on the football team and scores touchdowns. When Eric plays and scores Baylee cheers. When Baylee was very young she was invited to model clothes at a charity affair. After the show the outfit was given to her as a birthday present. Alexis (18 month younger sister) (Fig. 39) thought it all right for Baylee to wear the new clothes for the first four weeks and then it would be her turn to wear them. Baylee was asked how she learned to swim? Some friends dared her to go into the deep end. Baylee went into the deep end and splashed as hard as she could. That is how you learn to swim Bally once tried to take a bath in the toilet and was saved in the nick of time by her mother. Baylee thought it would be fun. She had taken off her clothes and ready for a bath. Thankfully her mother stopped Baylee in time.

Alexis recently graduated   from the 8th. Grade and will enter High School in the fall. She loves sports and was voted most valuable player on the basketball team 3 out of the past 4 years. This fall she will be on the varsity volleyball team at her High School. As a very young child Alexis invented her own language. Grandpa was Bobo, Grandma was Bobo mom, car was hum, Eric was Baka, and Puppy was Tee Tee, Daddy was Nana, Baylee was Yiyi, and blanket was hotty. The entire family learned to talk this language. After Alexis got older she learned English and started kindergarten at St. John's catholic school. Alexis broke her arm on the very first day of kindergarten, before her first class. Alexis fell from the monkey bars and broke her arm. Alexis said to her mother, "I told you that I shouldn't have gone to school." Grandpa and Grandma live in the county and Alexis loved to visit. Grandpa had two horses; Splash and Strawberry, both were gray horses (Figs. 40 and 41). Alexis would sit on Grandpa's lap and watch the horse races on television. Alexis cheered for every gray horse and shouted, "come on Splash, you can win!!" (Fig 42). During a drive to Grandpa's house with her dad and mother (Fig. 43) Alexis' mother asked Alexis to stop playing around or find another place to sit. The car was crowded with mother, dad and all the kids. Alexis looked around and asked, "Oh sure, where do you want me to sit, on the roof?

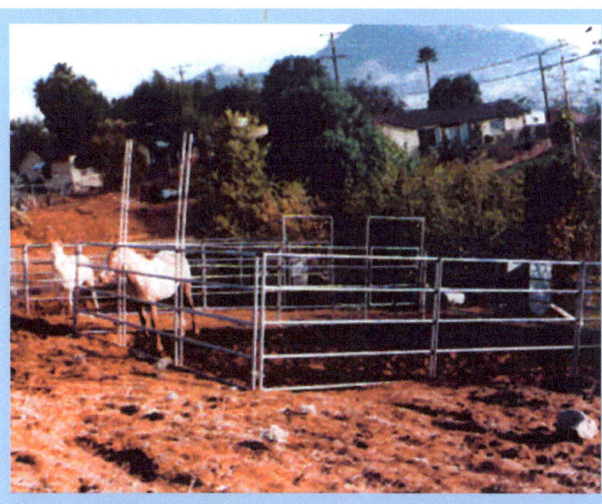

Figure 40. Splash and Srawberry Suzanne and Julie's horses

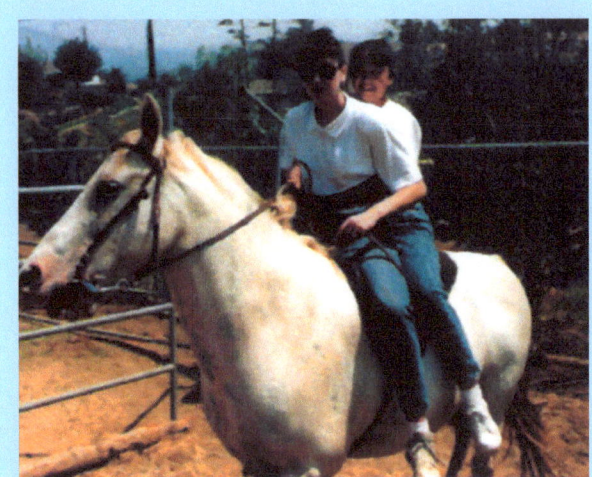

Figure41 Suzanne-and Splash

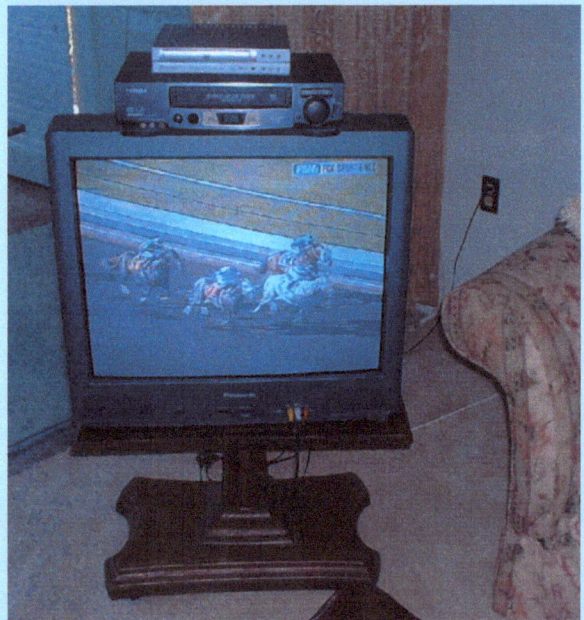

Figure 42 Horse races on television

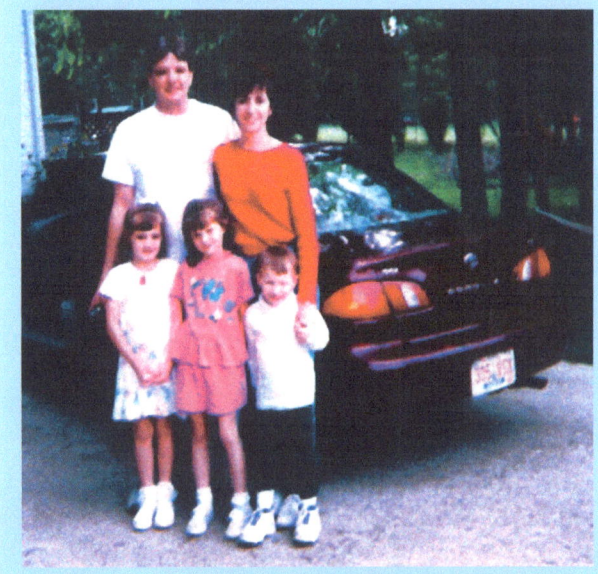

Figure.43 Suzanne:and John with Baylee, Alexis,and Eric

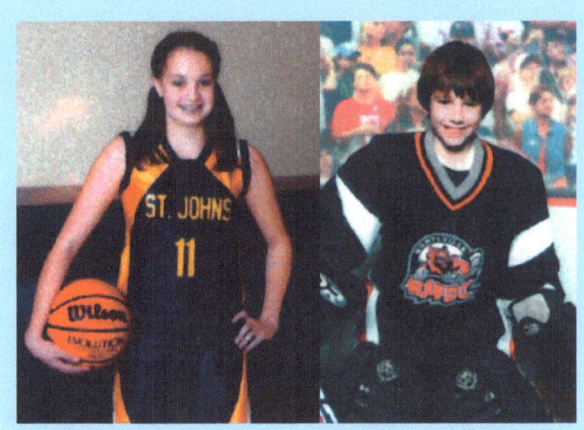

Figure 44 Suzanne's kids love to play sports

High this fall. Eric also loves sports, as do all of Suzanne's children (Fig. 44). This past season Eric was captain of his hockey team (Fig. 45) and the team won its conference championship. As a reward Eric was honored and asked to drop the puck to start the professional game at the Civic Center. There were over 4000 fans in attendance and Eric felt real pride

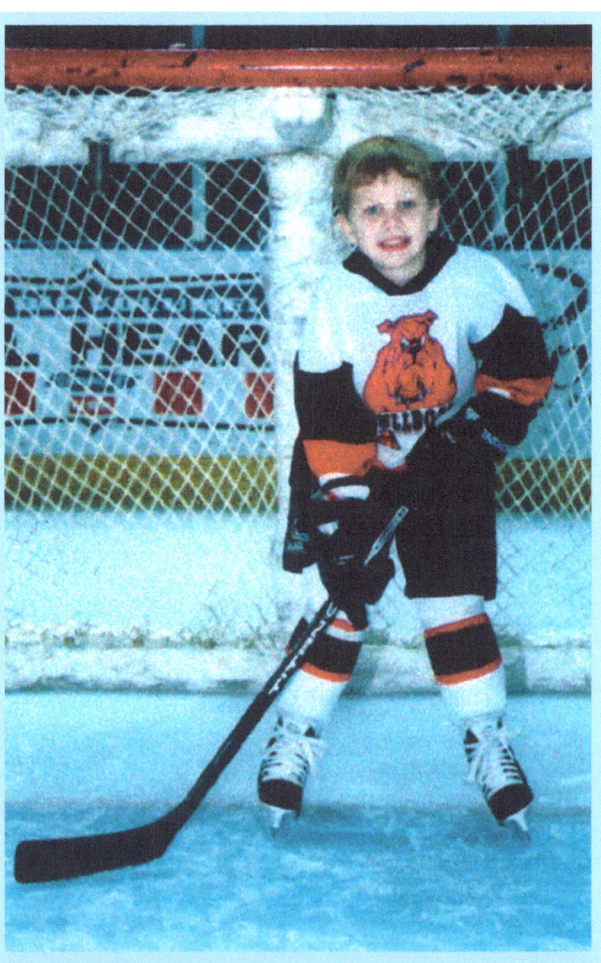

Figure 45 Eric captain of hockey team

name is Arthur. His mother told Eric that Grandpa's name is Arthur. Eric asked his mother, "was Grandpa named after me?' From then on, Eric was proud that Grandpa was named after him. Eric insists that they call him Eric Arthur. Eric scored his first hockey goal when he was 4 years old. This was his first game and it was exciting. No one told him which goal and Eric went to the wrong goal. When Eric finished kindergarten the girls loved him. One of the girls told Eric that someday she was going to kiss him. Eric's sisters overheard the little girl and teased him. Eric came home and told his mother, "The kissy kissy girls are at it again. Mother you have to do something about it!" His mother explained that it was a compliment. Later Eric told his mother that there was more than one kissy girl! Grandma always corrected the children if they had their elbows on the dinner table. Eric waited his chance and one night caught Grandma with her elbows on the table, Eric laughed so hard he almost fell off his chair! Suzanne and John (husband) have a family boat and they enjoy boating on a local lake (Fig. 46).

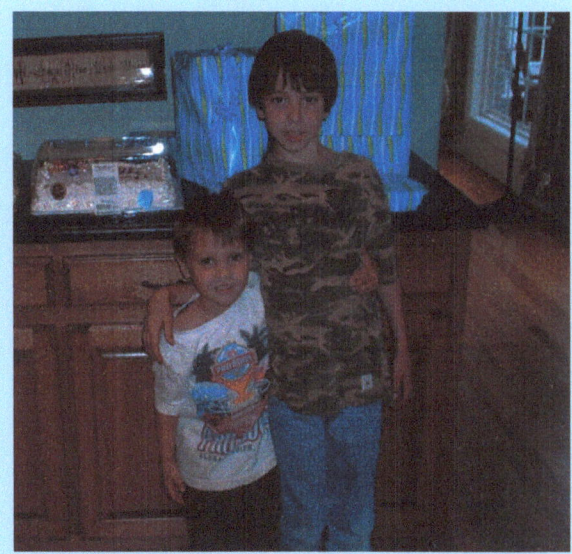

Figure 47 Sammy and Luke are pals

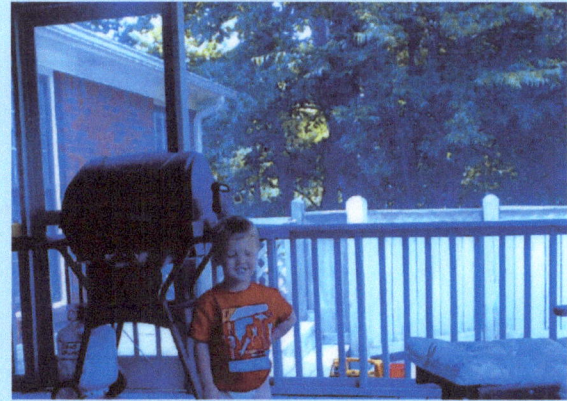

Figure 48 Luke on grandpa's porch

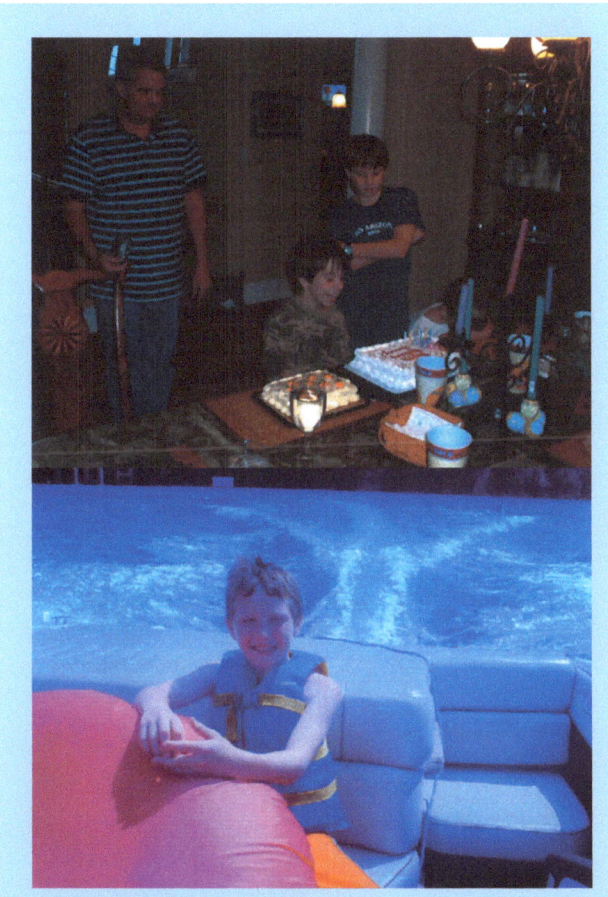

Figure 46 Eric enjoying a boat ride

Sammy (Suzanne's next to the youngest child) also plays hockey and loves to be the goally. Eric loved to tease Grandma and count up her mistakes. Sammy wanted to know many snakes Grandma had! Sammy didn't mean snakes but meant, "miss snakes." One day Grandma was visiting and Sammy asked her to play with him. Grandma was busy and asked him to wait a little while, after Grandma finished her work she offered to play. Sammy said, "you wouldn't play with me when I wanted to so now I won't play with you". Sammy loves music. One day Sammy got mad at his mother and asked her to "let me stay in my room and listen to music!" Sammy listened to music until he got over being mad.

Luke is the youngest (Figs. 47 and 48) and will be starting Pre School in the fall. Luke loves to go to McDonalds and get a hamburger (and a toy). His mother often tries to convince him that other restaurants serve hamburgers. In desperation Luke's mother will tell him that McDonalds is closed. Luke's respond is, **"You are fooling me"** or **"liar, liar your pants are on fire!"**

Part 6. Ending...

Mother and dad...

Mother and Dad had strong religious beliefs and supported their local Catholic Church. They celebrated their 50th wedding anniversary in 1961 in a subdued atmosphere since Dad had become ill with "Lou Gehrig" disease and was in the later stages of this terrible illness. Dad ran his business until the time of his death February 6, 1962. Mother died in 1971 from complications of liver failure having entered into a coma four months earlier.

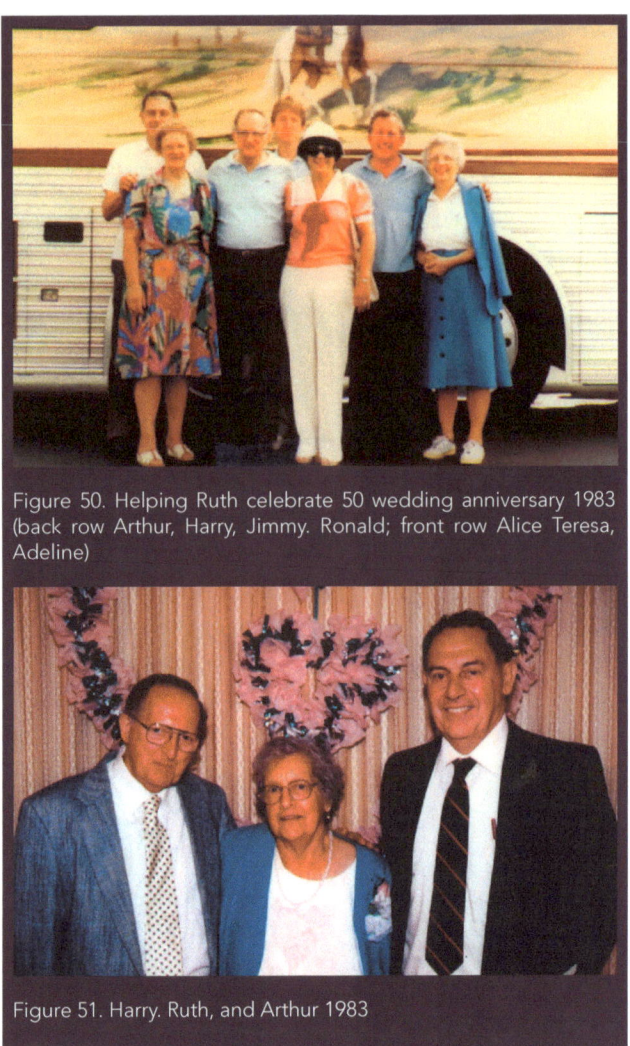

Figure 50. Helping Ruth celebrate 50 wedding anniversary 1983 (back row Arthur, Harry, Jimmy. Ronald; front row Alice Teresa, Adeline)

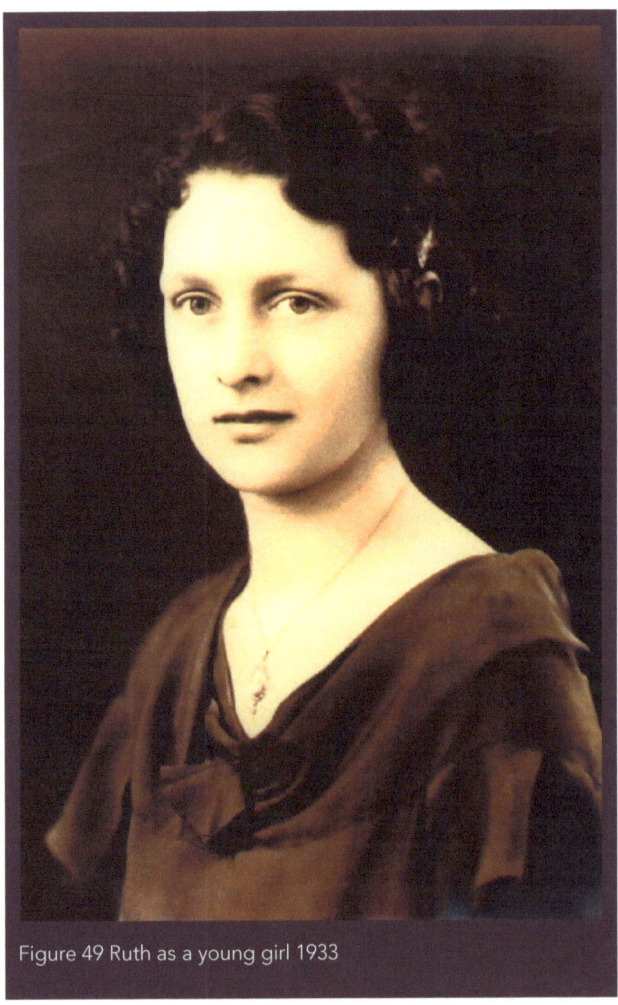

Figure 49 Ruth as a young girl 1933

Figure 51. Harry. Ruth, and Arthur 1983

Ruth first to marry...

Ruth (2nd oldest of our family) was the first to marry in 1933 at the time that I was four years old and Ronald one year old (Fig. 49). Ruth and Kenneth Drier celebrated their 50th wedding anniversary in 1983. It was a large celebration with the Drier family of seven children and sister and brothers, Adeline, Harry, Arthur and many friends in attendance (Figs. 50 and 51).

The war changed us...

World War II caused an early breakup of the Nussberger family. By the time that I reached my teens only Ronald and I were left living at home. The Nussberger's eight children settled in different parts of the country and Adeline is the only one that remains in Durand. Her daughter Corrine and seven grandchildren surround Adeline. Hubert died in 1947 in Sheboygan, Wisconsin and Andy Jr. died in 1991 in Tucson, Arizona. Ruth died at her home in Colby, Wisconsin in 1997. Ronald, the youngest of the Nussberger family, died on December 17, 2003 in Janesville, Wisconsin. Ronald was given a military funeral, having served in the Air Force during the Korean War. He is buried in Beloit, Wisconsin beside his wife, Teresa.

Family get together...

Rose Ann and myself take an occasional plane ride to visit Adeline in Durand. We often meet Harry and Alice in Las Vegas on vacation and there we enjoy a little gambling and entertainment. Family get togethers usually occurs at weddings which have been pretty regular since both Adeline and Ruth have many grandchildren getting married. Corrine, Adeline's daughter, raised a family of seven with six girls and we attended their weddings. Ruth raised a family of seven and currently her grandchildren are reaching adult hood and getting married.

Ruth visited Rose Ann and myself in California in 1996, a year before her death. She traveled by air with her son Robert and his wife Elva. It was a fun visit with Ruth enjoying the travel. She was thrilled by the airplane ride and enjoyed seeing some of the California sights. In 1997 Rose Ann and myself were in Huntsville, Alabama visiting our daughter Suzanne when we got an early Sunday morning call telling us that Ruth had passed away. It was a sad day. Rose Ann and I drove from Huntsville to the funeral in Colby, Wisconsin.

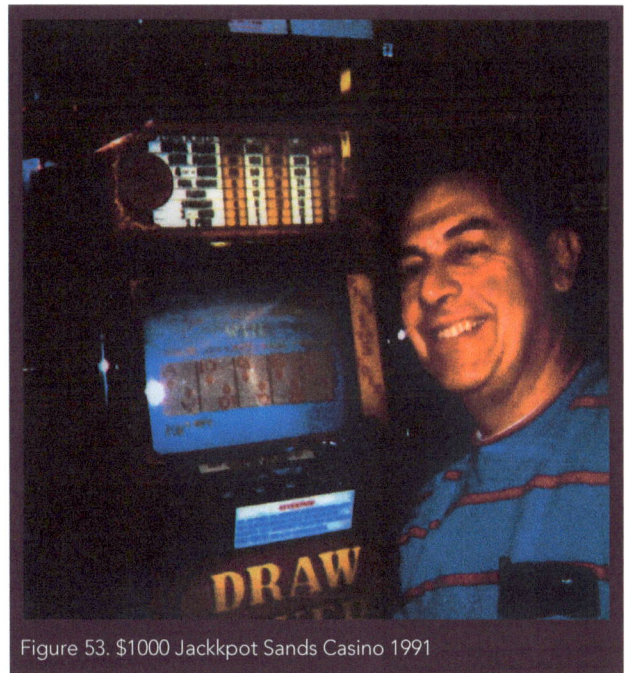
Figure 53. $1000 Jackkpot Sands Casino 1991

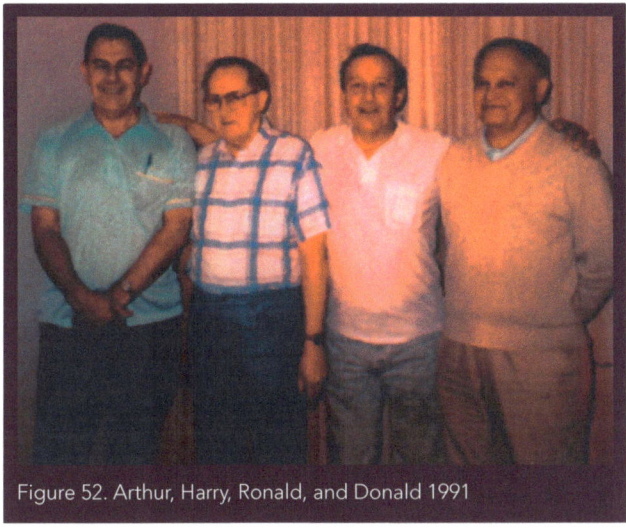
Figure 52. Arthur, Harry, Ronald, and Donald 1991

In retirement...

Donald, Harry, and myself are in retirement and remain in good health (Fig. 52). Donald lives in Tucson, Arizona, Harry in Sheboygan, Wisconsin, and myself in Riverside, California. Harry and his wife Alice celebrated their 40th wedding anniversary in Sheboygan, Wisconsin on June 18. 2000. We enjoy retirement and getting together and discussing our varied interests. Horse racing is a favorite subject along with grandchildren, and politics.

At times we have met Harry and Alice at Churchill Downs or one of the other racetracks for a few days of racing. At other times we meet at Las Vegas. Once in a while we get lucky and win. A big day was December 14, 1991 at the Las Vegas Sands (Fig. 53). **"Congratulations on your good fortune to be a winner of a $1000 jackpot!"** When that happens its celebration all around!

Growing up in a small town is a unique experience. The Nussberger children were all born at home with the assistance of Dr. Scott our family doctor. Dr. Scott came to Durand as a young man and spent the remainder of his life practicing medicine as a typical country doctor. I recall with fond memory Dr. Scott's farm a few miles outside town and as a teenager going with him in the evenings to the farm. Dr. Scott used these hours as a way to get away from the stress of his practice. Dr. Scott enjoyed spending a couple of hours feeding the animals and doing the chores or putting up fences. Our family home was a white frame house built in 1912 (Fig. 54) and located at the south end of Durand. The Chippewa River borders Durand and our house was located close to the banks of the river. I grew up spending a great deal of time along the river. Many summers were spent fishing on the river and in the winter walking along the bank trying to hunt game. I wasn't serious about either activity but enjoyed the experience of spending my time walking through

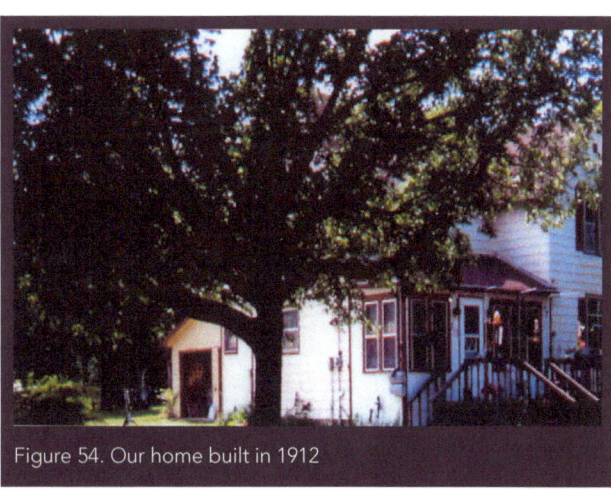
Figure 54. Our home built in 1912

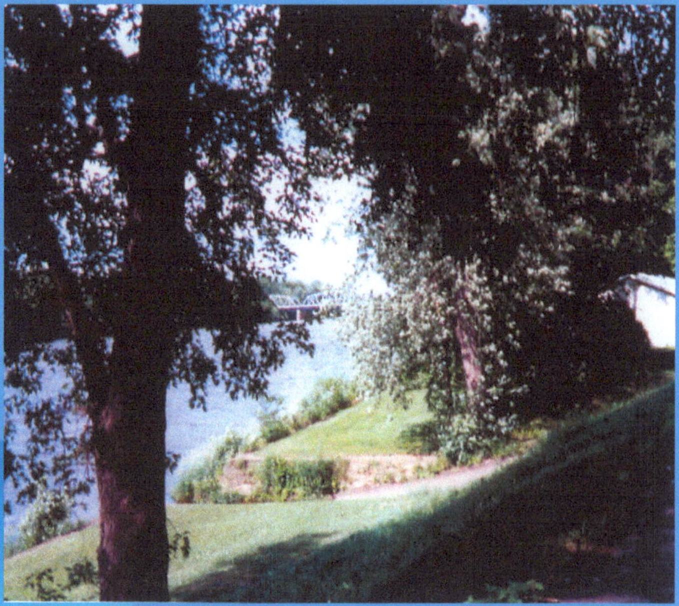

Figure 55. Along the banks of the Chippewa River

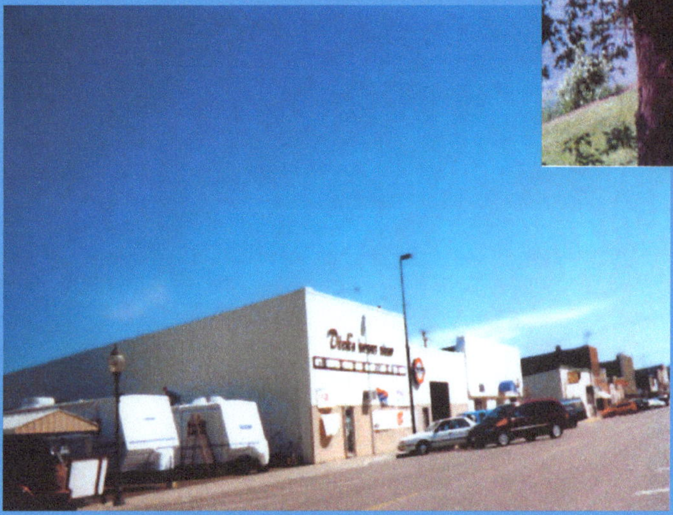

Figure 56. Main street Durand.

tranquility. All of the Nussberger children attended St. Mary's church and school. St. Mary's parish provided education for its children through the tenth grade. We were fortunate in that the school and church were located within easy walking distance from our home. The last two years were spent at Durand High located at the other end of town. Getting to Durand High was a little more difficult than going to St. Mary's since it was a long walk or involved borrowing Dad's car.

The winters in Durand were usually long and the only entertainment was the Durand Theater. Dad's shop was located at the south end of Main Street and the theater was located at the north end of Main Street. There were new movies shown on Sunday, Tuesday, and Friday nights. To get to the movies I would either walk along the riverbank or bicycle using the city streets. The town had constructed a wall along the river bank stretching from our end of town to the north end for flood protection. The wall was wide and provided a concrete walkway. Every spring the Chippewa River overflowed its banks and part of Main Street would be under water. Dad's shop would be immersed in water up to the first floor boards. The flooded streets would extend along the river very close

to our street at the south end of town. The ice melting caused the flooding and resulted in our finding a small canoe sized boat floating down the river. The boat was perfect for the river and it provided many relaxing hours on the river fishing or just drifting.

Growing up along the banks of the Chippewa River (Fig. 55) and in the small community of Durand was centered on home, church and school, the river itself, and down town Main Street (Fig. 56). When we graduated from high school we knew that this part of our lives were over and we had to move on. From the time we graduated from high school live would be different. The town wasn't big enough to support all of its grown children and most went to the cities for college or employment and few were able to return.

THE END

www.ingramcontent.com/pod-product-compliance
Lightning Source LLC
Chambersburg PA
CBHW040308010626
45792CB00025B/1626